# GETTING

CU00900946

# SPORT & LEISURE

Tony Charlton

TROTMAN   In association with   UCAS

First edition published in 1998 in Great Britain by
Trotman and Company Limited
– in association with UCAS –
12 Hill Rise, Richmond, Surrey TW10 6UA


© UCAS and Trotman and Company Limited 1998

**British Library Cataloguing in Publication Data**
A catalogue for this book is available from the British Library

ISBN 0 85660 376 7

Printed and bound in Great Britain by
Creative Print & Design (Wales) Ltd

# CONTENTS

# ACKNOWLEDGEMENTS

This book has been reliant on the goodwill, help and advice of a large number of people. Particular thanks are due to the UCAS institutions that supplied information on predicted entry requirements (see pages 65–88) that make such an important contribution to this book, and to my UCAS colleague Sylvia Crampin for her painstaking work in pulling together such a large amount of statistical data.

I also wish to thank Rosie Evennett from Liverpool Hope University College, Andrew Staffs from Cheltenham and Gloucester College of Higher Education, Lizzie Morrisey from Yeovil College and Karen Macdonald and Chris Weale from the University of Exeter, for describing their experiences as students on higher education courses, and Keith Haynes, John Parker, Peter Thompson, Richard Carroll and Claire O'Brien for generously giving of their time to talk about their working lives.

# INTRODUCTION

This book does not contain a magic formula for how to become a Premiership football manager or, for that matter, how to earn a million pounds a year as a professional sportsperson. What it does do is provide an overview of an employment area that is set to offer an ever-increasing range of work possibilities in the 21st century. However, no one should minimise either the competitive nature of the job market or the competition for entry to relevant higher education courses.

Thorough research is always a key to success. At interview, whether for a college place or a job, it is usually the individual who can display more than a superficial knowledge of the subject, along with enthusiasm and commitment, who succeeds. This book provides a range of background information that, when linked to college visits and further reading, will give you an excellent awareness of sport and leisure-related employment possibilities.

## Student views

Dotted throughout this book are the views of students. When asked, several wished that such a publication had been available when they were at school to make them more street wise about choosing a college course. Despite the diversity of personal interests and lifestyles, several common denominators can be discerned.

- A high level of personal commitment
- A real sense of fulfilment in being able to combine physical and intellectual skills in the context of daily study and work ('not so much a career as a way of life' was a typical comment)
- An awareness that their chosen vocation is, like law, medicine and media, a highly competitive job market.

## Setting realistic goals

That sport plays a significant part in most of our lives is indisputable. Major events, like racing's Grand National, attract thousands of live spectators and, from the TV companies' viewpoint, attract millions of armchair viewers. Our everyday language includes many sporting allusions – 'the news hit me for six' or 'I was pipped at the post for promotion', for example – and many newspaper readers turn straight to the back page, the traditional home of sports reporting, before looking at other sections. Our dreams, too, are not immune from images of sporting prowess as, up and down the land, winning goals are scored in World Cup finals, Wimbledon finals are won with unstoppable serves and athletic track world records are shattered by unbelievable amounts!

Given this all-pervasive presence, it is not surprising that sporting heroes are role models for many young people. But the truth is the world of professional sport, as experienced by the majority of players, is far removed from the glamour, fame and fortune achieved by the chosen few. For every sportsperson who achieves his or her goal of participating at professional level, there are thousands of 'wannabees' who, despite bags of enthusiasm and commitment, fall by the wayside. Their sporting participation will probably be played out in the more homely surroundings of the local sports centre, dry ski slope or Sunday morning football league. However, as this book aims to point out, significantly more people work in leisure-related sport activities than earn a living as professional players.

As ever, the key to achieving a personal goal lies within each individual. This requires, as a starting point, a totally honest self-assessment of what attracts him or her to the subject. To opt for sport and leisure, as a career, purely because it sounds 'fun' (or, hypothetically, could make someone very rich) is naive in the extreme; if an individual unadvisedly does so, the only thing likely to be scored is a demoralising 'own goal'. That is what this book seeks to avoid.

## Who is this book for?

*Getting into Sport and Leisure* offers guidance to anyone attracted to the possibility of working in sports or associated leisure fields. While prospects in many careers will be strongly enhanced by higher education qualifications, it is important to stress that people who, for a diversity of reasons, do not wish to undertake higher education are not barred from working in this field. As well as essential data for students assessing their suitability for a career in sport and leisure, the career paths and student profiles will be helpful for teachers and careers officers, as will the the review of higher education courses and useful addresses for gathering and maintaining up-to-date information.

The book has no upper age limit for readership and can therefore help older individuals interested in entering this field, whether currently employed or unwaged, to build up an initial source of information.

# GETTING UP TO SPEED

No prospective entrant to the sport and leisure employment field could complain about lack of choice. Before focusing more closely on courses and careers, it will be useful to examine the concept of 'leisure', the structure of professional sport, some of the attributes you will need to study at higher education level and, in addition, some ways of gaining initial work experience.

## ☐ THE LEISURE INDUSTRY

Like many words in the English language 'leisure' has gained new meanings in the last 30 years. Although the dictionary definition of 'free time; time at one's disposal' is still relevant, more often it crops up in two-word phrases like 'leisure industry' and 'leisure centre'. In the past, individuals and families would primarily organise their free time themselves, often at little cost or distance from the family home; now we increasingly pay others to provide services and facilities for our use away from our home, study centre or work place. When we book a squash court at the local leisure centre, pay for windsurfing tuition or enjoy a day-trip to a theme park we are, like millions of fellow Britons, participating in the leisure industry. This, of course, is good news for the one million plus people who are now employed in the sport and leisure sector.

The growing emphasis on healthy lifestyles has led to an upsurge in the number of people looking to keep themselves fit. While in the 1970s and 1980s jogging was very popular, statistics show that increasingly many people join fitness classes or a gym for the social interaction rather than (as is often the case in jogging) the solitary approach to keeping fit. In order to cater for the huge upsurge in interest, sports centres and gyms have sprung up in towns and cities throughout Britain, either as new construction projects or as a conversion of an existing building. Some are private and some are council owned, but all need qualified instructors to run the huge variety of classes and activities that take place on a daily or weekly basis.

## Strong interest

An interest in sport is fundamental, as is an awareness of its key role in improving the health and general well-being of people. Your interest must be totally genuine and stand up to close scrutiny by experienced admissions tutors (be warned, sports lecturers have a sixth sense that can sniff out anyone who thinks it is just one big excuse to play their favourite sport all day!) *'Get real'*, advises an experienced admissions tutor:

> *'Research what lies behind the course titles well before you apply. As a high-demand higher education subject, which sports studies is, most colleges and universities are in the happy position of having many more applicants than places available. For example, we usually have ten applicants for every place, some universities have double that number. As a result, we can afford to be very selective about making offers.'*

## One way to start

One practical way of getting an inside look at employment in sport and leisure, and earn some money at the same time, is to train to become a swimming pool attendant at your local leisure centre. As a pool attendant, it is obviously vital for the well-being of the general public that you are properly qualified which, as a minimum, usually means gaining the Amateur Swimming Association's (ASA) certificate in life saving. A growing number of students gain this certificate while studying for qualifications like A-levels/Scottish Highers, Advanced GNVQ or Edexcel/SQA diplomas, working a manageable number of evening or weekend hours around their academic studies. As the safety of the public is paramount, you will probably find that being a pool attendant can be mentally tiring due to the high levels of concentration that must be maintained.

## Networking

A buzzword of the 1990s, 'networking' simply means making contacts and the passing of information between people with mutual interests. For example, working at a mountain bike, ski or surf shop will bring you into contact with a lot of sport and exercise oriented people; in turn, this will increase your chance of finding out about other job possibilities and, as likely as not, provide you with several first-hand accounts of what studying sport at university or college is really like.

# ☐ PROFESSIONAL SPORT – THE FACTS

Along with the weather, sport is a subject which features prominently in many everyday conversations, in every city, town or rural village. Just look at the millions of votes annually cast in the BBC's competition to find their 'Sports Personality of the Year'. The winner, as likely as not, has already earned a considerable amount of money from his or her sporting prowess and, when finished as a player, may then go on to forge a second career as a TV personality.

It seems glamorous, but to get there usually calls for tremendous dedication and, owing to the demands of high-intensity training, the sacrifice of the sort of social life which most teenagers enjoy. Along the way they will have risen up through the ranks, starting with school representation, followed by district and county and, if very lucky, a schools international. They will have acquired a coach and made contacts with their local sports officials and, from an early age, will have become aware of the burden of expectancy that youthful promise often brings. As a professional they will have confronted two facts of sporting life: first, a sporting career as a player is unlikely to exceed 10–15 years and, second, paying spectators are the worst of critics, and very fickle – they can and will voice their disapproval if they feel levels of performance are below par or on the wane.

The world of sport can be very cruel and unforgiving. At 11 years of age, for example, you could receive rave notices as a playground footballer, but by 14 or 15 your dream could have crash landed through a persistent injury or, more likely, through losing out to the sheer weight of young people who are determined to succeed in the scramble for fame and fortune. For every professional sports player who achieves their dream, there will be thousands who never make the transition from promising amateur to a paid sporting performer. That disappointment may be considerable to ambitious young sports people, but many go on to gain the educational and vocational training required to work in one of the careers described later in this book. Meanwhile, some successful professional sports people, due to the demands of their sport, neglect their general education and, at the end of a short career, have no qualifications to offer a potential employer. As one ex-footballer ruefully comments:

*'I left school with no qualifications and a head full of dreams about making it as a professional footballer. Which I did – although 11 of my 12 seasons were spent in the third division playing in front of*

*very small crowds. My one season of glory, if you can call the first division that, gave me a couple of Scandinavian players as team-mates. Most of us had messed up in school (the only British player with an A-level was nicknamed Einstein!), so it was much to the amazement of the dressing room that our European team-mates had gained qualifications in teaching and accountancy before taking up full-time professional football. Looking back, I realise that they were the smart guys, as they had qualifications to fall back on after their playing days were over. Apart from some sporadic scouting work, my lack of qualifications make my immediate job prospects bleak.'*

## ☐ NATIONAL GOVERNING BODIES

In Britain each major sport has its own national governing body (NGB). To progress within a sport, it is important not to transgress any of the rules of the NGB and, for coaching careers, it is essential to acquire the various qualifications offered by the governing body. In total, over 100 sports are recognised and funded by the Sports Council and they are a good place to start for information about a particular sport. Examples include the British Amateur Gymnastics Association, the National Ice Skating Association and the British Ice Hockey Association. In an overarching role, the United Kingdom Sports Council, formed on 1 January 1997, promotes the development of sport and fosters the provision of facilities for sport and leisure through funds (originating from the Department of Culture, Media and Sport) to individual NGBs.

Funds from the National Lottery are distributed by the separate English, Welsh, Scottish and Northern Ireland Sports Councils (see Useful Addresses, page 89).

## ☐ UNIVERSITY OR PRIVATE SECTOR TRAINING?

For some careers (eg medicine) it would be inconceivable to qualify to practise the profession from a private sector training course. However, in a growing and competitive industry like sport and leisure there are a large number of private sector organisations that specialise in meeting the demand for vocationally trained staff. The vast majority of private sector courses are considerably shorter than the average degree course and therefore do not pretend to mimic the content of a higher education course, but concentrate on teaching the vocational skills needed for a particular job.

Many students who enrol for a private sector course (say, in sports therapy or fitness instruction) do so after having completed a first degree in sport and leisure. Although a degree course will give you an excellent grounding in the subject and, in terms of skills valued by employers, will greatly enhance your ability to problem solve, think flexibly, source information and communicate effectively (both verbally and in writing), most sport and leisure degree courses operate on a generalist rather than an overtly vocational basis. So it is important to get vocational training to supplement your theoretical knowledge.

## Contemplating a career change?

If you are looking to change careers, an intensive vocational training course that provides essential workplace skills and does not tie up three years of your life may well appear an attractive proposition. Someone who has been working and earning for a while is likely to consider the financial benefits, such as loss of earnings minimised etc. However, it is still a big investment, so don't get carried away by the marketing claims. Before signing up, look carefully at the qualifications on offer, the accreditation, the facilities for students and the provider's reputation.

In conclusion, most teachers and careers advisers would promote higher education, in terms of long-term career and salary benefits, as being the preferred option for young people with suitable entry qualifications. However, if carefully chosen, the private sector has a number of training organisations that operate with the highest level of professionalism and are well respected in the sport and leisure industry. On a practical note, no student loans are available for private courses and, to meet costs, many students take out a Career Development Loan (CDL).

# TYPES OF COURSE

Given the tremendous interest in sport and leisure activities in the UK, it is not surprising that colleges and universities offer such a wide range of courses catering for a variety of student requirements. At first glance the titles of some of the courses in the UCAS *Handbook* can appear confusing, as the language used may be unfamiliar. Under 'Sport', for example, relevant courses include Sports Studies, Sport and Recreational Studies, Sports Sciences, Exercise Sciences, Physical Education, Sports Medicine, Fitness Science, Coaching Science, Outdoor Studies, Sports Product Design, Sports Management. Likewise, under the heading 'Leisure' can be found an equally large number of courses, including Themed Leisure Management and Design, Technology for Leisure and Recreation, Adventure Tourism, Adventurous Activity Management and Outdoor Recreation Management.

This is not an exhaustive list, merely an illustration of the index of possibilities available to the prospective student. The main categories of higher education qualifications are as follows.

## ☐ SINGLE HONOURS

For entry in 1999, there are 1134 degree courses available through UCAS at British colleges and universities. Many of these courses receive large numbers of applicants; some, particularly at institutions with worldwide reputations, are among the most competitive in the whole of British higher education. For example, a well-known BSc (Hons) in Sport, Coaching and Exercise Science, during the 1997 UCAS application scheme, received 1200 applications for 90 places. That sort of ratio of applicants to places is prevalent at several other colleges and universities.

As a general rule of thumb, almost all single honours degrees that focus primarily on sports sciences will expect, as an entry criteria, a science qualification at A/AS, Advanced GNVQ or Edexcel National Diploma level.

# ☐ COMBINED/MODULAR DEGREES

In common with subject areas like media studies and business studies, the number of combined and modular degree programmes exceed the number of single honours options and, in total, provide a huge menu of study possibilities. Examples include Sports Science and Russian (University of Wales, Bangor), Early Childhood Studies with Sports Science (Canterbury Christ Church College of Higher Education), Sport and Exercise Science with Computing (Nottingham Trent University), Human Resources Management and Sports Sciences (University of Stirling) and Leisure Management and Tennis Studies (Buckinghamshire Chilterns University College).

# ☐ SANDWICH DEGREES

A minority of sport and leisure courses include paid work experience built into the course structure. A 'thick sandwich' usually means two years at college/university, one year's employment, and, to conclude, one year back at college/university (four years in total). In a 'thin sandwich' the work experience is spread in three-month or six-month blocks throughout the four-year degree.

# ☐ HIGHER NATIONAL DIPLOMAS (HNDs)

Usually of two years' duration, with work experience as an integrated component. In England, Wales and Northern Ireland courses are validated by the Edexcel Foundation (BTEC); in Scotland, validation is the responsibility of the Scottish Qualifications Authority (SQA). Courses are available, on a far less frequent basis than degree provision, in subjects like sports science, leisure studies, sports coaching, health and fitness, recreational management and sports injuries.

# ☐ DIPLOMA OF HIGHER EDUCATION (DipHE)

When available, which is not often in this subject area, a two-year course with the option to progress (via another year's study) to a degree. The Credit Accumulation and Transfer Scheme (CATS) means that credits from awards, like the DipHE, are recognised by the vast majority of British higher education institutions. So, from a student viewpoint, this is a particularly flexible qualification as it makes it possible to 'top-up' the DipHE into a degree, at a time that suits, and, if desired, at another institution.

# ☐ POSTGRADUATE QUALIFICATIONS

In line with many other university degree subjects, there are growing opportunities to take postgraduate qualifications. Mirroring the situation at undergraduate level, many courses either focus on sports sciences or sports administration. There are also opportunities to study leisure and recreation management at a number of colleges and universities. Because of funding restrictions, a significant number of students undertake postgraduate studies after a period of employment subsequent to their first degree and, in increasing numbers, on a part-time basis. For intending teachers of Physical Education, the postgraduate certificate in education (PGCE) provides qualified teacher status and awards are available from the Department for Education and Employment. There are also opportunities to study for the research degrees of MPhil and PhD at some universities.

# CHOOSING YOUR COURSE

Your ability to absorb, hold and recall information will be tested to the full in choosing a suitable course. Why? Because no other European country has anywhere near the range of sport and leisure higher education courses offered in Britain. The first part of this chapter focuses on the different types of institution that offer courses. The second part is an in-depth look at the factors that are important to consider when weighing up which course, at which university or college, is best for you.

## ☐ 1. THE INSTITUTIONS

### Universities

With the exception of a small number of long-established universities (eg Birmingham, Brunel, Exeter, Glasgow, Leeds, Loughborough), the majority of university course provision is at institutions that acquired university status in 1992/93. This includes many former polytechnics (eg Anglia Polytechnic University, University of Central Lancashire and University of Portsmouth). Some 1960s 'technological' universities (eg the Universities of Bath, Brunel and Loughborough) have a long track-record of offering courses in sports studies. Taken overall, university provision veers towards theoretical aspects of the subject which, for entry purposes, can have implications for the sort of educational attainments which admissions tutors require (see Entry Routes, page 24).

### Colleges of higher education

These colleges often started life as specialist teacher training colleges and through subsequent mergers may have widened their range of courses but, despite growth, they remain involved in the training of PE teachers. They offer a wide variety of courses. Although single subject degrees can be found, a marked feature of this type of institution is the opportunity to study for a combined or modular degree. Examples include Canterbury Christ Church

College of Higher Education and Cheltenham and Gloucester College of Higher Education.

## Colleges of further and higher education

Sometimes very large in terms of student numbers, but with the majority of students studying on further education courses, this sort of institution is different from the other categories because there is a great likelihood that the majority of students will be living at home. Examples include Barnsley College and St Helens College.

# ☐ 2. FACTORS TO CONSIDER WHEN CHOOSING A COURSE

Because there are a broad range of factors to think about, UCAS consulted a panel of lecturers, higher education sport and leisure students and professional coaches and administrators for their comments. They came up with a whole alphabet of advice:

**A** is for **Add-on Costs**. The sorts of things that might not be listed in the prospectus but that will make inroads into your funds, as a student, studying on a particular course. For example, if the course has any practical sports component, you will need to buy sportswear and, for the sake of your fellow students, keep it clean! Remember, one pair of specialist sports shoes can sometimes cost the equivalent of half a dozen CDs.

**B** is for **Building**. British higher education is offered in a multitude of building styles, old and modern. A prospectus boast of high-tech sports facilities may, in reality, turn out to be true in part (say, good equipment) but, on the downside, be blighted by leaky roofs or erratic heating systems. As one long-suffering student put it:

*'My university sports facilities include state-of-the-art weight training and fitness laboratories, gymnasia, tennis courts, running track and a large indoor swimming pool, which is all to the good. Unfortunately, the showers are dodgy and the heating and ventilation system seems permanently at odds with the weather outside.'*

**C** is for **Competitions**. Student sport can often achieve very high standards and national competitions are keenly fought by teams

13

and individuals from all over Britain. Don't be shy. Find out how the institutions that interest you have fared in recent years. Some universities have created sports training villages which, due to their superior facilities, attract top-class athletes who previously would have trained abroad because of inadequate facilities in the UK. The presence of élite athletes in turn acts as a strong marketing point for generating higher education applications.

**D** is for **Depth.** No, not a reference to the deep end of the swimming pool but to the depth of teaching expertise (and facilities) available within an institution. Laboratories, gyms and field and track facilities need properly trained technician and groundsman support to function properly. As one student ruefully commented:

*'My research into diet and lifestyle management was disrupted by the long-term absence through illness of a key technician and the subsequent problems that the university encountered in providing cover for her post.'*

**E** is for **European Exchanges.** Some sport and leisure courses may offer opportunities to undertake part of the course at a college or university in Europe. If this appeals to you, be sure to target institutions that have proven links with European colleges and universities; in addition, ask questions about funding arrangements and accommodation.

**F** is for **Food**. Good nutrition is at the very heart of exercise and health promotion. If visiting an institution, check to see if the canteen has a menu more varied than burger and chips!

**G** is for **Governing Bodies.** A feature of the British sport scene is that most sports operate within the strictures of their own national governing bodies and, historically, have supervised their own training qualifications. This has important job implications for graduates who wish to earn a living as an instructor or coach within a particular sport. For example, a sports degree by itself will not automatically enable someone to become a canoeing instructor. To do this, a graduate would need to satisfy the relevant governing body, ie the British Canoe Union (BCU), that he or she has the necessary technical competence.

**H** is for **Halls of Residence**. If you are an only child, suddenly moving into a college or university hall of residence means adjusting to sharing kitchens and other facilities with a lot of others. How many rooms does the college or university have for first-year students (some guarantee a place for all first years). If not sited on the main campus, how far away are they? Is there a frequent (free) bus service?

**I** is for **Interview.** If asked to an interview for a place on a course, what sort of questions will you be asked? The answer, whatever the degree, is that the admissions tutors will be looking to see if you have something more than a skin-deep interest in the subject. Think about the following questions – how would you set about answering them at a college or university interview?
1. Is there a link between sporting and academic ability?
2. Why do so many young women drop out of sport?
3. How would you slant an anti-smoking and healthy lifestyle campaign aimed at 13–16-year-olds?

**J** is for **Jobs.** A growing number of students set about choosing a higher education course on the basis of what kind of job will materialise at the end. As mentioned earlier, the sport and leisure industry has benefited from the general public's growing awareness of fitness, health and lifestyle issues. Lecturers are aware of potential applicants' concerns over employment prospects and, if asked, will often be able to give details of student destinations. But do bear in mind that the primary function of many higher education courses is not to provide direct vocational training, so it may be necessary, depending on your desired career, to undergo further training.

**K** is for **Keyboard Skills.** Basic computing skills are as important for a sport and leisure student as they are to students in other subject areas. When reading about or visiting a college, check to see what sort of computer facilities are available; remember, also, that the Internet is a fantastic source of information and can keep you up to the minute with developments on the other side of the world.

**L** is for **Library**. Why is it that prospectus photos always manage to show well-stocked shelves with just one or two students browsing at leisure? The reality can be very different, with key books on short loan only, a dozen students occupying every table and a queue to use the hard-pressed computer facilities for CD-ROM viewing. In addition to checking the stock of books, academic journals, periodicals and magazines, you may find the library has an interesting archive of sports-related images (old college or university team photographs, newspaper clippings). Spare a little time for these – it is interesting to see the changes in sporting performance and participation in our present century, and useful to understand how the industry has developed.

**M** is for **Management Skills.** Sports administration and management is a career area that has really come of age in the last 20 years and it has opened up new employment possibilities. Although an increasing number of higher education applicants are looking for specialist courses in this field, others will gravitate towards administration and management from coaching, the armed forces, teaching, health and exercise promotion backgrounds or, indeed, after spending their twenties and thirties as professional sportspeople.

**N** is for **Numbers.** No one should make an application through UCAS without taking time to conduct some research on the relative popularity of individual courses. To help, look in the latest edition of UCAS's *University and College Entrance: The Official Guide* (most schools, colleges and careers companies have a copy) for information on entry requirements. Courses that attract large numbers of applicants will usually reflect this in the level of entry requirements that you need to match to gain a place.

**O** is for **Open Days**. Although it will involve expenditure on travel, most people would strongly advise going along in person to take the measure of an institution's facilities. UCAS annually produces an *Open Day* booklet (see page 23) that can help you pinpoint the relevant dates for your diary. As one lecturer comments:

*'Committing two or three years of your life to a course is a big decision, probably the biggest that you have made so far in life. We want you to get it right. Therefore it makes good sense to come along and meet us rather than put all your trust in the prospectus, or the recommendation of a friend, workmate or relative.'*

**P** is for **Physical Education.** 'PE' to generations of school students, and a foundation subject in the National Curriculum. While every secondary school has a mandatory requirement to have a specialist PE teacher, the primary sector has no such requirement although recent developments, spearheaded by the Youth Sports Trust, aim to have in place sports activity programmes for every school in the country by the year 2000.

**Q** is for **Questions.** Thorough research is the key to ensuring that you do not end up on a course that is the opposite of what you really want. 'Sport', as a shorthand title, covers a wide variety of specialisms. Some of these courses have a high science content, others place greater emphasis on personal sporting performance or educational theory. If visiting a course, talk to as many students as possible. Ask them about staff/student ratios. How many sporting clubs are run by the university? How is your work assessed? Are modular degrees really flexible, or is that just prospectus hype? Ask if their tutors have a wide range of teaching and research experience in the fields of physical education, health, exercise, leisure management and sport.

**R** is for **Resources.** There is obviously a limit to how much you can see and do on a half-day's visit to a college or university as a prospective student. Some sports-oriented resources are hard to miss – eg pitches, swimming pools and weight training suites – but, looking closer, you may find that some facilities are off-limits to students at certain times of the week because they are booked by outside organisations or clubs. Also, are the facilities gathered together in one central place or dispersed over several campuses?

**S** is for **Scientific Principles.** To understand the principles that lie at the heart of modern teaching and coaching methods in sport, it is vital to be able to absorb specialist information from fields like physiology, biomechanics and kinesiology (the study of human movement), psychology, anatomy and sociology. If you and science are sworn enemies, look elsewhere for something to study!

**T** is for **Teaching.** An ex-name from the world of professional sport on the staff may be impressive, but previous expertise as a player does not automatically make him or her a good teacher. Also, members of staff who are highly thought of for their research skills may, as lecturers, lack the communication skills to enthuse students at their lectures, seminars, sports coaching clinics or in the laboratory. The increase in student numbers participating in higher education has inevitably led to a cut in the amount of time that a member of staff can spend with individual students. However, significant developments in the use of information technology means that students do not necessarily suffer from less face-to-face contact with their tutors. For example, reading lists and teaching materials can be published on an institution's computer network and interactive tutorials between members of staff and students can take place using the Internet. All higher education courses must make themselves available for inspection by the Quality Assurance Agency for Higher Education (QAA). If assessment has taken place, ask to see how the standards of teaching, resources and student support and guidance were rated by the QAA.

**U** is for **University Status.** What's in a name? University status does not automatically confer any extra quality to a course. As most undergraduate courses in this subject area are not overtly vocational some employers will be looking for additional qualifications (see V below), rather than offering a job purely because a student attended a particular university.

**V** is for **Vocational Qualifications.** The exercise, health, sport and leisure industries, in line with other areas of professional work, require nationally recognised qualifications for career advancement. Public concern over safety standards has led to a streamlining of qualifications within the NVQ framework. If you are unable, for whatever reason, to contemplate taking a higher education course for two or three years, there are bona fide companies that specialise in providing training courses for the health and fitness industry. Be realistic in your expectations. Despite claims that you might see advertised in some literature, a weekend course with a bit of home study attached is clearly not going to give you the sort of accredited qualification that will impress corporate and public sector employers. At all times (and before handing over any money for fees), reassure yourself the course is approved and validated by national awarding bodies.

**W** is for **Written Assignments**. Most courses use a variety of assessment methods, which may include essays, assignments, multiple-choice tests, presentations, competence tests and laboratory reports. Due to inadequate research, some applicants forget this and think, misguidedly, that their days will be spent in a tracksuit, playing sport morning, noon and night.

**X** is for **Xmas Holidays**. How much will travel cost between your family home and the college? Some triathlete PE students have been known to cycle up to 100 miles home at holiday periods; the majority of students will probably forgo that pleasure!

**Y** is for **Yardstick.** Try to visit a number of colleges and universities for comparison purposes. If this proves impractical, remember that the UCAS website (see page 89) has links into most college and university websites and continues to offer an expanded range of services to potential students, parents and teachers.

**Z** is for **Zest**. As many of the careers in this field call for at least a modest level of fitness, it goes without saying that if you come over as a couch potato (in your UCAS application form or at an interview) a place is unlikely to be forthcoming. Of course, universities do not expect you to be a TV Gladiator and, indeed, for most courses there is no need to have reached a high level of sport achievement, but you do need to convince admissions tutors that you have the necessary physical and mental stamina to complete the course successfully.

# SOURCES OF INFORMATION

Before filling in any application forms, you need to know as much as possible about the institutions and courses you are considering. The previous chapter discussed factors to take into account when you are making your selection, here we look at different ways of sourcing information:

- Teaching staff
- The prospectus
- Alternative prospectuses
- Reference books
- Videos
- Multimedia (UCAS website)
- Higher education 'Next Step' fairs
- Personal visits
- Skill: National Bureau for Students with Disabilities.

## ☐ TEACHING STAFF

If you are still at school, start with your PE or sports teachers. Ask them about their experience of college or university life. If their student days were 15 or more years ago, there is a strong chance that the institution they attended has undergone a name change. For example, many Welsh PE teachers received their training at the former Cardiff Institute of Education (now part of the University of Wales Cardiff) in the southwest, St Luke's Teacher Training College is now part of the University of Exeter; while in the East Midlands, the former Loughborough College of Education is now part of Loughborough University.

Despite name changes there will still be much that is relevant today – for example, if you are interested in developing your practical skills in a sport, as a student you will need to strike the right balance between that and the course's theoretical work. Your teachers will have encountered this during their student days and may be able to give guidance with the benefit of hindsight.

# ☐ THE PROSPECTUS

Every college and university prospectus invariably follows a similar format. It usually starts with a short welcome from the Director, Principal or Vice-Chancellor, goes on to describe the charms of the host town or city, then names and describes each course, department by department, with statements on aims and objectives, resources, methods of teaching, student assessment and entry requirements. It may give an outline of career opportunities (due to space restrictions, rarely more than a paragraph or two) and, more and more often, some case studies of recent students. There will also be sections dealing with student union activities, welfare, accommodation and – of particularly relevance to you – sporting facilities.

College and university prospectuses are often produced by marketing and external relations experts who always seem to have remarkably similar ideas about what attracts prospective students. According to many teachers, the end product can appear somewhat samey and, in their relentless upbeatness, too good to be true. On the other hand, they are *free* and are still the best starting point in helping you make your choice of institutions for the UCAS application form.

# ☐ ALTERNATIVE PROSPECTUSES

A growing number of student unions produce alternative versions of their college or university prospectus. Usually oriented towards the social side of student life, adverts for bars, clubs, music and fashion shops tend to predominate, and they are unlikely to contain detailed course descriptions. Nevertheless, they may still provide a useful role by 'telling it like it is' about the sports facilities, both on campus and in the host town or city.

# ☐ REFERENCE BOOKS

Your starting point should be the UCAS publication *University and College Entrance: The Official Guide,* which will give you information about subject requirements, likely offer levels etc. In addition, you may find it useful to read *Careers in Sport* by Louise Fyfe (Kogan Page), and, as many sport and leisure careers are linked to tourism, *Questions & Answers: Tourism* (Trotman).

# ☐ VIDEOS

Videos were all the rage not so long ago but are now used much less as a marketing tool by universities. Your school or college will probably have some reference copies or you can ask to borrow them from the institution.

# ☐ MULTIMEDIA (UCAS WEBSITE)

Increasingly course information is available on CD-ROM and, for most colleges and universities, via websites on the Internet.

The UCAS website provides an interactive map showing the location of all member colleges and universities, together with their contact details and profiles of their student populations. A course search facility helps potential applicants undertake an initial search for courses and institutions, and provides information on all courses recruiting through UCAS. Whether you want details of course availability in a particular region or want to search more generally, selections can be made by subject area (eg sports studies/sciences), course level, mode of study and other criteria, such as expected grades. To provide maximum usefulness, links are available directly to the websites of UCAS institutions, giving a wealth of information about course provision and life as a student in particular towns and cities. You can access the UCAS website by opening your Internet browser and typing: http://www.ucas.ac.uk.

# ☐ HIGHER EDUCATION 'NEXT STEP' FAIRS

These are held in most parts of the country, starting in March and going right through until the end of the summer term. Designed primarily for Year 12 students (ie first year A-level or equivalent), they provide an ideal opportunity to speak to representatives from the majority of UCAS colleges and universities. They are like big trade fairs and are an ideal place to pick up prospectuses – and pick the brains of the higher education representatives. Most representatives will be the official schools liaison officer for their institution and therefore have to be generalists, so don't expect to meet a specialist sports studies tutor on every university stand that offers the subject, but do ask, as some events will have academic representatives from sport and leisure departments.

Most schools and colleges take parties of pupils to their local Next Step event, but if nothing is being organised for you through the school, you can always go independently with a group of friends.

# ☐ PERSONAL VISITS

A recurring theme in this book is the desirability, whenever possible, of only applying to institutions that you have personally visited. Of course, this will have cost implications for you but, as things stand, there really is no substitute.

Most institutions hold at least one Open Day a year and, to help, UCAS annually produces a booklet *Open Days, Pre-taster Courses and Education Conventions*. This contains a complete set of dates for college/university Open Days and taster courses. (It also lists Next Step higher education conventions, mentioned above.) Copies are distributed free of charge to schools, colleges and careers companies. If you have difficulty in locating a copy, contact UCAS direct (see Useful Addresses, page 89).

Before a visit, you need to prepare a list of key questions about facilities, costs – check out the A–Z on pages 13–19 for the factors you should think about.

# ☐ SKILL: NATIONAL BUREAU FOR STUDENTS WITH DISABILITIES

This is a national voluntary organisation working to develop opportunities for young people and adults with disabilities and/or learning difficulties. Skill acts as a national resource for students with disabilities, their families and teachers who work with them. It can provide information on institutions that have created special sporting facilities for disabled students – for example, University of Wales Institute Cardiff. (See Useful Addresses on Page 89.)

# ENTRY ROUTES

The well-prepared applicant knows that thorough research is the key to success. Put simply, you need at your fingertips details of subject requirements, likely offer levels etc before listing your choices on the UCAS form. This chapter focuses on entry requirements and looks at the types of qualifications applicants are likely to have. To illustrate how grade or point scores can vary enormously from institution to institution, see pages 65–88 for the 1999 expected requirements for sport and leisure. **This information is for general guidance only. Institutions may change requirements for a variety of reasons and may make higher or lower offers to individual applicants.** At all times, check with institutional websites and prospectuses before finalising your choices.

## ☐ 1. ACADEMIC

### GCE A-level/AS

GCE A-level is currently the main qualification in England, Wales and Northern Ireland for entry to sport and leisure related degree courses, accounting for 59% of UK entrants in 1997. It is also accepted for entry to Scottish institutions, and it is not uncommon for applicants from England, Wales and Northern Ireland to study in Scotland.

An A-level in Sports Studies or Physical Education is not a mandatory requirement, although such qualifications will obviously indicate that you are someone with prior knowledge of the subject. In general, any combination of A-levels will be acceptable, although some degree and HND courses – for example Sports Sciences – will want to satisfy themselves that you can cope with the laboratory based scientific modules and you should therefore find a science A-level (say, Biology) particularly useful. Modular A-levels are increasingly popular among students and, for application purposes, have the same status as linear A-levels for entry to college and university courses.

You may wish to apply for a higher education place offering AS qualifications as well as A-levels. Most institutions will accept two AS-levels as the equivalent to one A-level. As a ready reckoner, you can translate A-level/AS grades into point scores as follows:

| Grade | A-level | AS-level |
|-------|---------|----------|
| A | 10 | 5 |
| B | 8 | 4 |
| C | 6 | 3 |
| D | 4 | 2 |
| E | 2 | 1 |

Your overall achievement can therefore be expressed as a score. Institutions may make you a conditional offer based on actual grades, eg CCC, or on an overall points score, eg 18 points, in which case they may also require a specified grade in one of your A-levels.

## Scottish Highers/Certificate of Sixth Year Studies

Scottish Highers are the usual academic entry qualification offered by Scottish applicants, many of whom choose to study at Scottish colleges and universities for their higher education. Most institutions in this book will require a minimum of three Highers (commonly four or five) and may specify a particular grade in some subject. Scottish qualifications are readily accepted by colleges and universities in England, Wales and Northern Ireland, but some may additionally require passes in the Certificate of Sixth Year Studies.

## Access Courses

Colleges and universities welcome applications from mature applicants (ie over 21 years of age) particularly if, before applying, they have completed an access course kitemarked by an Access Validation Agency. UCAS and the Quality Assurance Agency (QAA) have developed a database which gives details of access courses that are available in further education colleges and universities.

These courses have a common framework offering key skills and study skills as well as subject-specific units. The database can be consulted in many careers offices, adult guidance units and higher education institutions. Are you considering applying as a mature student? If so, the free UCAS booklet *The Mature Student's Guide to Higher Education* will provide a lot of useful information.

## Irish Leaving Certificates

Most colleges and universities will accept the Irish Leaving Certificate for entry purposes.

## European/International Baccalaureate

Most colleges and universities will accept a good performance in the European or International Baccalaureate.

# ☐ 2. VOCATIONAL

## Edexcel Foundation BTEC/Scottish Qualifications Authority National Diploma

There are a large number of vocational diploma courses which, although developed to prepare people for a variety of leisure and sports-related jobs can also, if required, be used to apply for higher education courses. Some courses, particularly those with a high written content, may require an additional A-level or AS/Scottish Higher, in addition to your national diploma.

## General National Vocational Qualification (GNVQ)/General Scottish Vocational Qualification (GSVQ)

Advanced GNVQ and GSVQ level 3 are accepted for entry to higher education. Information on expected entry requirements, for guidance purposes, is given on pages 65–88 and (in greater detail) the latest edition of *University and College Entrance: The Official Guide*. Although there is not a named GNVQ in Sport, many Leisure and Tourism GNVQ students will be interested in the type of higher education courses highlighted in this book.

## National Vocational Qualification (NVQ)/Scottish Vocational Qualification (SVQ)

These vocational qualifications are based on work-based assessment of particular skills, and they are assuming increasing importance in the fields of sport, leisure and outdoor education. Students may wish to apply for a higher education course holding an S/NVQ qualification in an area like coaching and instructing, outdoor education, sports development or facility management (for example, having managed a fitness and health club). S/NVQs can be offered alongside academic or other vocational qualifications.

## Other qualifications

Depending on the course you intend to apply for, other qualifications can be deemed acceptable for entry purposes. For example, for a degree in sport and leisure management an applicant may hold a vocational qualification like the City & Guilds Certificate in Recreation and Leisure Industries or, alternatively, a certificate or diploma from the Institute of Leisure and Amenity Management (ILAM).

# MAKING YOUR UCAS APPLICATION

This chapter does not set out to tell you every last detail of making an application, but highlights the major points of which you should be aware. For more detailed guidance refer to the UCAS *Handbook* and/or website, the instructions accompanying your UCAS application and the various documents that will be sent to you subsequently by UCAS.

## ☐ WHAT IS UCAS?

UCAS is the Universities and Colleges Admissions Service, the organisation that handles admissions for over 250 British colleges and universities. If you want to study for a sports or leisure management degree for application purposes you must fill in a UCAS form.

## ☐ WHAT ARE YOUR CHANCES?

Like law, medicine, media studies and art and design, sport and leisure are very popular subject areas with many courses attracting large numbers of applicants. In 1996/97, 11,543 applicants applied for courses in Sports Science/Studies, of whom 10,007 were under the age of 21. Of these applicants, 3444 were accepted to study sports science/studies, including 83% who were under 21.

Turning to leisure studies, in 1996/97 10,681 applicants applied for courses in leisure and associated studies, of whom 9000 were under 21. Of these applicants, 2778 were accepted to study the subject, including 76% who were under 21. By December 1997, 18,500 applicants had applied for sport and/or leisure courses in the 1998 UCAS scheme.

Remember that the level of competitiveness varies considerably from institution to institution, and that it is in your interests to research this thoroughly before filling in your UCAS form.

# ☐ THE UCAS APPLICATION FORM

You may make up to six choices on your UCAS form. A significant number of students choose to list only sport and leisure choices although, of course, you will not be penalised if you list alternative course choices. When listing your choices, the golden rule is not to appear less than committed by including too wide a range of choices. An experienced admissions tutor comments:

*'Although the majority of applicants make choices which are coherent, I sometimes see at interview students who give off mixed messages because of the lack of logic in their choices. I am also very keen to weed out any applicant who might view my sports science course as a second-best solution if they fail to be offered a place on something else, say, a physiotherapy course.'*

## Electronic applications to UCAS

UCAS has developed a system called the Electronic Application System (EAS) which has now been offered to all schools and colleges. It allows you to apply to UCAS using a standard personal computer rather than fill in a paper-format form. If your school or college is using the new system you will be given full details by your teacher, tutor or careers adviser.

# ☐ HOW MUCH DOES YOUR APPLICATION COST?

Whether using the paper form or applying electronically, the standard fee is £14. However, for applicants who only wish to apply to one institution, eg if you are a mature student limited to one particular institution by family commitments, there is a reduced fee of £5 for one choice.

# ☐ YOUR PERSONAL STATEMENT

The personal statement (Section 10 of your UCAS application form) is your golden opportunity to bring your application to life by listing your achievements and interests. Before setting out to do so, please remember that when your form arrives at UCAS it will be copied and reduced in size before being distributed to your chosen institutions.

Therefore, if your handwritten personal statement is virtually illegible full-size it will be totally impenetrable when reduced and will make as much sense to admissions tutors as Egyptian hieroglyphics! The golden rule, as ever, is to work your ideas through on practice copies (by photocopying the form) rather than launch straight into the real thing.

When presenting information about yourself, you should take note of the things listed elsewhere in this book that sport and leisure tutors are likely to be looking for. You do not need to use all the space available and, indeed, conciseness can often produce a much snappier, more focused, piece if writing.

If you have a National Record of Achievement, this will be valuable as a starting point for presenting a clear account of your achievements and interests. You should make clear your motivation and commitment and, if applying solely for Sports Science/Studies courses, make it clear to the admissions tutor that you are going into this with your eyes open and – this is a crucial point – you are well aware that the course is not just one endless session of playing sport. You should give information about your interests, activities and achievements, particularly any coaching or instructor qualifications which you have already gained or any sporting achievement (say, being picked for your county's youth side or being invited to join a training camp for promising young sports people).

This is your big opportunity to sell yourself to admissions tutors, but you should do so honestly without exaggeration or distortion. A highly experienced admissions tutor comments:

*'In practice some of our applicants undersell themselves, either by poor presentation or by omitting important information that would have assisted their case. Others, in contrast, get carried away when listing their achievements and end up implying that they can play football better than Pele or, in tennis, blow Steffi Graf off court. For our sports coaching degree specialisation, one applicant filled most of the personal statement with a lengthy account of how moved he had been by the role of the coach in the 1980s film* Chariots of Fire. *If he had been applying for, say, film studies this mini essay might have gone down well, but it was way over the top for us!'*

There is no ideal or recommended way to structure your personal statement. This is because admissions tutors, as a group, are made up of thousands of individuals who share the common goal of finding the right students for their courses but, in preferences, will vary from subject to subject. An experienced admissions tutor comments:

*'From a personal viewpoint, I find it easier to digest an applicant's statement if it is broken up into paragraphs or by headings. To help my decision-making, I want to learn about things like your reasons for choosing sport and leisure, the depth of your interest in the subject and any relevant work experience, paid or voluntary, which is relevant to the subject. This will also be the ideal place to list key skills developed through, for example, GNVQs, GSVQs, NVQs and Modern Apprenticeships, if applicable to your application. In addition, be sure to include details of any achievements in sporting or leisure pursuits that you have gained (whether as a participant in a particular sport or as a coach, supervisor or instructor) eg Diploma of Achievement or the Duke of Edinburgh's Award. But please, above all else, keep a sense of proportion. I am not going to be impressed by a sports studies applicant whose sporting achievements appear to go no further than winning an egg-and-spoon race as a boy scout!'*

# ☐ TIMING YOUR APPLICATION

The normal UCAS closing date for receiving applications is 15 December. As pointed out elsewhere in this book, many courses receive many more applications than places available, and start their selection process as soon as they receive their first applications from UCAS in October. Although some teachers and lecturers recommend the early submission of forms, every UCAS institution will, all things being considered, give equal weighting to all applications that reach UCAS by 15 December.

# ☐ SELECTION CRITERIA

The criteria used to decide whether or not you should be made an offer will vary from one institution to another. In general they are likely to take into account some or all of the following factors:

- Your existing academic qualifications, eg at GCSE or equivalent, with, say, for Sports Science particular reference to Science and Mathematics.
- Your current programme of study, eg GCE AS/A-level, Scottish

31

Higher, Advanced GNVQ, Edexcel diploma or Access, with particular reference to the subjects you are offering in relation to the specific entrance requirements for the college or university concerned.

- Your referee's prediction of your likely performance in forthcoming examinations/assessment.
- Evidence of your suitability for Sports Science/Studies from your personal statement, including details of coaching or instructor badges and relevant work experience (eg pool lifeguard).
- If applying for a sporting scholarship (see page 37), evidence of your sporting prowess.
- Your referee's confidential statement.
- If called, your performance at interview.

For school and further education-based applicants, it is highly likely that your academic credentials and grade predictions will be the most important initial factors, the other considerations coming into play only if you are of a suitable academic calibre.

Sport and leisure departments vary in their policies over interviewing. While some will interview a substantial proportion of applicants, others will only interview applicants with certain circumstances, eg mature applicants, those resitting exams, and those applying from overseas. Some departments will use existing students as part of the interview process, although often with observer-only status, which will, if nothing else, ensure that someone very close in age to you is also in the interview room.

Many schools and further education colleges take very seriously the need to rehearse students for higher education interviews, holding 'mock' sessions using past questions etc, but although extremely beneficial it cannot totally replicate the real thing. Your mock interview is going to take place in the familiar surroundings of your school or further education college, which is very different from undertaking a journey from your home to a college or university and, once there, walking into an unfamiliar room to convince a group of strangers (ie admissions tutors) that you are worth a place.

Common sense suggests that you need to keep abreast of recent sport and leisure-related topics, eg the sort of stories making the major national newspapers or appearing on television. For example, there has been a lot of media coverage on the illegal use of drugs to enhance sporting performance – athletics, cycling and weight lifting come to mind – but other sports have also received coverage. As an applicant, you may be asked to comment on this highly topical issue. How would you set about expressing your views?

# ☐ AFTER YOU HAVE FILLED IN THE FORM

After completion of pages one, two and three of the UCAS form it is ready to be passed to your referee, who completes a reference for you on page four. In schools, this is often the head teacher, who draws on school records and the opinions of your subject teachers. For mature applicants, however, it may well not be a viable option to approach previous schools; as an alternative, you should ask a professional person who knows you well for a more recent account of your skills, achievements and personality.

References are treated very seriously by higher education because they provide insights into your motivation, personality and ability to study with others. The referee's view of your thought processes, powers of expression (both oral and written) and ability to engage in self-directed study, coming from a fellow educationalist, will have an influence on an admissions tutor's decision on whether to offer you a place or not. Once completed, the form with enclosed fee should be sent to UCAS by 15 December. If you apply by this date you are guaranteed consideration. If you apply after, the institutions will only consider you at their discretion.

UCAS will check your form, acknowledge it, and send reduced-size copies to all the institutions to which you have applied. Your chosen universities and colleges will be considering your application at the same time – some may interview you, but interviews are becoming less common except for subjects like Physical Education Teacher Training where they are compulsory.

If you are taking qualifications (such as GCE A-levels, Scottish Highers, an Advanced GNVQ or Edexcel BTEC diploma) you may be made a **conditional offer**. This simply means that you will be set certain grades to achieve, or, in the case of A-levels, perhaps a point score. If you have already obtained suitable qualifications for entry, you may be made an **unconditional offer**. If you accept this, please note that this firmly places you on that course and therefore makes your other choices redundant.

# ☐ WHAT IS CLEARING?

UCAS annually operates Clearing from the middle of July until September to fill the remaining places in colleges and universities. As results are announced at different times – ie GNVQ and Access in July, Scottish Highers early August, A-levels in mid-August – the scheme runs for almost three months. As an applicant, you are eligible to enter Clearing if:

- You did not receive any offers from your original application, or
- You turned down any offers you received, or were not accepted because you failed to meet the conditions of the offers you were holding, or
- You submitted your application after 30 June.

If eligible, UCAS automatically sends you a Clearing Entry Form (CEF). In Clearing the onus is on you, as the applicant, to do the legwork. Vacancy information is available from a variety of sources such as *The Independent*, the UCAS website and CEEFAX on television. Once you have found a vacancy that interests you, go into action (don't write, ring them direct).

In 1997 over 54,000 people got themselves placed at the Clearing stage, but some places in higher education still went unfilled. However, don't expect to find vacancies in Clearing for the more popular Sports Studies courses.

# ☐ TAKING A YEAR OUT

A feature of the last ten years has been the growing popularity of taking a year out before entering higher education. To help shape your thinking, a 'Year Out' exhibition stand is now available at all the UCAS/Next Step network of higher education fairs. This has been sponsored by a number of organisations and covers teaching abroad, participating in a cultural study exchange, adventuring on the other side of the world, working in industry and learning a foreign language.

Whatever you choose to do, admissions tutors will expect you to make an effective use of your time and, as they were not there with you, will be interested in a full explanation on your personal statement.

You should apply in the same way as for normal entry, but indicate in Section 3 of your form that you are applying for deferred entry. If all goes well you will be offered a place and, once confirmed, can take your year out secure in the knowledge of a place waiting for you when you return in the following autumn.

# MONEY MATTERS

Making ends meet is obviously a vital part of being a student. Beginning in 1998/99, the maximum means-tested grant for a student will be reduced, in line with government recommendations, and there will be a corresponding increase in the size of the maximum student loan available. There will be an initial means-tested contribution to tuition fees of up to £1000 a year. The government estimates that less than 40% of students will have to pay the full £1000 and, for students from lower income families, tuition will continue to be free.

Queries about both grants and tuition fees should be made to your Local Education Authority (LEA) as early as possible. Application forms are normally available from Easter onwards.

## ☐ STUDENT LOANS

From the year 1999/2000 the maintenance grant will be totally replaced by student loans.

You can apply for a loan after you have taken up your higher education place at your college or university. You will need to present a birth certificate, evidence of your bank or building society details, your student registration card and evidence of your LEA award letter.

From your viewpoint as a student, no loan repayments will have to be made until you start to earn a salary in excess of £10,000 a year. Graduates in employment who earn above this level will pay off the loan by making regular contributions from their salaries (at the time of writing, probably by the Inland Revenue deducting at source through its tax codes). The total annual parental contribution to fees and maintenance combined is intended not to be any higher than the contribution paid by parents towards maintenance under the existing system.

The above information was correct at the time of publication, but may be subject to change dependent on government policy. A free booklet on *Financial Support for Students* is produced by the Department for Education and Employment (DfEE); it can be ordered by calling 0800 210280 or by e-mail: info@dfee.gov.uk.

# ☐ MIXING PART-TIME WORK WITH FULL-TIME STUDY

It is now almost the norm for students to supplement their grant and loan income by having a part-time job while working towards a higher education qualification. All of the students profiled in this book (see pages 56–64) were asked, with particular reference to preparing for examinations, for their comments on balancing the demands of a part-time job and study. Not surprisingly, the general view was that it would be far preferable for students to have sufficient income not to have to work but, to be realistic, part-time jobs were here to stay. As one student commented:

> *'The trouble with work is that it is very tiring and, in my case, pool life-guarding is doubly so because of the need for constant poolside vigilance. On the upside, it is all relevant experience in the sport and leisure field, but getting up to supervise an early morning swimming session for the public is sometimes very difficult, believe me.'*

# ☐ SCHOLARSHIP

Sports scholarships are awarded by some universities and colleges for particular prowess. By the time of a higher education application, this will have already been recognised through representational sporting honours at various levels (county, regional and perhaps even national). It also probably means that you have been a member of a sports club and, in support of your application for a scholarship, can use a coach connected with the club or an official from your sport's governing body as a referee.

For a successful applicant, scholarship can offer a number of advantages beyond the obvious one of extra cash, including a one-year extension of the degree, free coaching and sports injury clinics, a car parking permit (on many campuses, worth its weight in gold!)

and help with travel to sporting competitions. Although athletics scholarships tend to predominate, places are also available for a range of other sports including hockey, golf, rowing, rugby and tennis.

Institutions offering scholarships include Bath, University of Wales Institute Cardiff, Exeter, Loughborough and Northumbria.

## ☐ SPONSORSHIP

The thought of finding a company or organisation to sponsor you as a student may sound enticing, but in reality it happens to very few students. Sponsorship, when available, is likely to carry certain obligations, such as working for that company for an agreed length of time after graduating or during your student holidays.

# CAREER PATHS

This chapter looks closer at a selection of sport and leisure-related job possibilities. To reflect the real ratio of opportunities, this book deliberately places the emphasis on work in fields like coaching, teaching, outdoor pursuits instruction, groundsmanship, sports centre management, sports photography and sporting equipment design. Clearly, no prospective entrant to the sport and leisure field could ever complain about lack of choice. For the career-minded, there are literally dozens of options and it should be remembered that for every career featured in this book, there are several closely related but separate careers that, given the space, could equally have been included.

## ☐ COACHING

To get the most from a sport, no matter how much latent talent you have, access to a coach is vital. This is particularly crucial when starting out, as it is very easy to pick up bad habits that will, if left unchecked, limit the level of success to be gained from participation in a particular sport. This holds true right across all sporting activity and therefore offers a wide range of work opportunities for coaches with recognised qualifications. Every sport, almost without exception, has its own governing body which administers training opportunities for coaches at all levels.

Most media coverage of coaching in professional sport has tended to focus on football, rugby, cricket, tennis and athletics, but in the 1990s there are coaching opportunities in a host of other sports, including water sports (surfing, canoeing, sailing, swimming and diving), golf, basketball, ice hockey, tennis, squash, winter sports (skiing and snow boarding), climbing, bowls, archery and judo. Taking a lead from football, where many coaches are ex-players who have played the game at a professional level, many other sports have examples of those who have turned to coaching after their playing careers have ended. Sport and leisure is, of course, an area of work that extends way beyond the confines of professional sport.

### Related careers

Opportunities exist for working with local authorities in sports development schemes, outdoor pursuits and adventure holiday centres, private gym and leisure companies, or in an administrative capacity for a national governing body.

# ☐ PE TEACHING

Everyone reading this book, whether still attending school or not, will have their own memories of PE lessons as, by law, it is a National Curriculum subject that must be available to all pre-16 pupils. Think of a secondary school PE teacher and, as often as not, an image comes to mind of a man or woman, probably under 40, and wearing (unlike the rest of the teaching staff) track suit and trainers. What might not be so readily apparent is that their training route is identical to other subject areas, that is, requires a degree, and will take a minimum of three years in higher education to achieve qualified teaching status.

There are two routes into PE teaching. The first, which requires a commitment to teaching at the point of commencing higher education, is to take a Bachelor of Education (BEd) degree. The second, which is preferable for those who wish to leave their options open, is to choose a degree of obvious relevance to PE teaching (as outlined on page 9) and, once completed, to take a further year of study to gain a Postgraduate Certificate of Education (PGCE) in Physical Education. Entrants to the teaching profession should be aware that the basic requirements for these courses include GCSEs in English and Mathematics (if born after 1978, a GCSE in Science is also required). Not surprisingly, an interest in (and aptitude for) playing sports will be very helpful. Be warned, however, sporting prowess by itself will not be sufficient to become a qualified teacher in a primary or secondary school.

### Related careers

Opportunities exist in the Armed Forces, the Police and the Prison Service for Physical Education instructors. At primary school level, where teachers are generalists rather than specialists, teachers with a PE/Sports Studies degree background may be asked to coordinate the school's overall physical education programme alongside their normal classroom teaching.

CLAIRE O'BRIEN – PHYSICAL EDUCATION (PE) SECONDARY TEACHER

From my GCSEs onwards, my career plan was to work in the leisure industry or to become a PE teacher. I had always been keen on sport and had, in fact, played netball for my region.

To get into higher education, my teacher and careers officers advised me to study a GNVQ in Leisure and Tourism. This included units in sports psychology and sports coaching and, during work placement, I spent a total of six weeks working in two sports clubs attached to schools. By the time of my higher education application, I had come down in favour of teaching, so I applied for a number of teaching courses. After some initial setbacks, due to some institutions feeling that GNVQ was not an appropriate qualification for teacher training, I was accepted by Sheffield Hallam for the BSc honours degree course in PE with Education, which carried Qualified Teacher Status (QTS). Looking back, I would alert anyone wishing to go this route to be well aware of the need for a sound grounding in science (I'd studied biology and chemistry at GCSE), as otherwise a subject like biomechanics will prove very challenging.

When I graduated, gaining a second-class honours degree, I moved quickly into my first post as a sports teacher at Howard of Effingham School in Surrey and, what's more, at an enhanced salary because of my honours degree. Thanks to the seeds sown by my GNVQ (which was very hot on good time-management skills), I have coped very well with organising and prioritising my time as a teacher.

It's been said many times, but teaching offers rewards which far exceed the amount of money you are paid, as a bonus for the PE teacher, there are ready-made facilities to keep yourself up to speed with your own sport and in a good state of general fitness. The excellent facilities we have, thanks to a successful lottery bid, are appreciated not just by our pupils but, in the evenings, by local people who participate in a range of courses like aerobics and fitness training.

My school offers a range of lunchtime extracurricular activities and, as a county standard netball player, I naturally lead a club for that sport. As the youngest teacher in the school – I was just 21 when I started – I also have the advantage of being very close in age to many of my pupils. Hopefully this puts me on the same wavelength as them, rather than being bracketed as part of their parents' generation.

Most of my out-of-school time is devoted to netball. As a centre or wing attack I regularly play for the county side, both home and away, and recent fixtures have taken us up to Merseyside and down to Bournemouth on the South Coast. My involvement with the sport also includes getting involved in development work within the region.

The All England Netball Association, the national governing body, is keen to increase participation in the sport and, locally, I have been involved in skills clinics for young people. Part of the problem, whether for netball or physical education in general, is that many teenagers give up on exercise and sport due to peer pressure and, as a result, at school level we increasingly encounter problems of overweight and uninterested children. For sport at representational level, development work is important because it ensures that young talent can be fostered and nurtured through the teenage years so that, at county level, fresh young talent can emerge.

To be realistic, life as a teacher can be very demanding, both physically and mentally, but I have no regrets in taking up teaching as a career.

# ☐ FITNESS TRAINING

The continual expansion of the fitness and training industry means a constant demand for instructors and personal trainers throughout Britain. This category includes aerobics and aqua fitness, where exercise is conducted to music, as well as activities using weight training and gymnasium programmes. Whatever activity you choose to teach, it is vital that you can plan and safely deliver fitness programmes for individuals and groups. To do this needs proper vocational training and, increasingly, fitness instructors look to the private training sector to equip them with the necessary skills for employment. Apart from local authority sport and leisure centres, opportunities exist to work in the thriving private sector sport and leisure market, in large hotels, on cruise ships and, as a freelancer, for private individuals and corporate clients.

If you wish ultimately to work for yourself in this field, you will need to develop good marketing and business skills in order to survive in the very competitive job market. The public expects a fitness trainer to be properly qualified and people are unlikely to be impressed by someone who thinks they are the 'finished article' after one or two weekend training courses! However, as mentioned elsewhere, the very fact that you have, say, a three-year degree in sports studies does not by itself qualify you as a fitness instructor. Indeed, many gyms and sports clubs will want confirmation of essential workplace skills before employing someone as a weight training instructor.

### *Related careers*
Sports psychology and nutrition are areas of work that a fitness trainer could, given suitable training, choose to specialise in. Hospitals, for example, increasingly employ qualified nutritionists to give advice to patients on all matters related to diet and, in the world of professional sport, the links between performance and diet are taken very seriously.

### RICHARD CARROLL – FITNESS TRAINER

I went to school in Dublin and left at the age of 15 in pursuit of vocational qualifications in the field of recreation management and fitness instruction. After an initial training course in Dublin, I moved across Ireland and took a two-year Diploma in Sports Science at Galway University. Like many a student before me, in Ireland or wherever, I found the money situation very tight and the only way to survive was to work part time in a local leisure centre as a lifeguard.

The Galway course was 85% geared towards theory and, as one or two of my fellow students found to their cost, a lack of sound maths could make the going very tough. Thankfully, my maths held up and, bit by bit, I started to understand the scientific principles underlying sport and exercise performance. Compulsory modules covered anatomy, biomechanics, physiology and psychology.

After completion I spent a summer earning some money on Jersey then, at the end of the season, moved over to England and went along for a job at a David Lloyd Centre in Bournemouth. David Lloyd was just about Britain's biggest male tennis star in the days before Tim Henman and Greg Rusedski, representing Britain in the Davis Cup and playing regularly at major events like Wimbledon. Upon retiring from tennis, he launched a successful career as a businessman owning a string of sporting centres that, while providing indoor courts for promoting participation in tennis, also offered a range of other facilities.

In terms of my main interest, fitness training, I soon came to realise that certain qualifications were particularly well respected by mainstream employers like the David Lloyd organisation. Although my Diploma showed that I had a certain level of technical ability, I needed something extra to prove I could use it in the workplace with real clients. This coincided with a radical restructuring of training in the field of sport and recreation, led by concerns over safety, and the subsequent development of NVQs that covered a range of relevant competencies. After consultation, I took out a career development loan and enrolled with Premier Training & Development, a nationally recognised training provider, to gain a coaching NVQ. My thinking was that if I successfully completed the course, it would be a passport to working anywhere in Britain in the sport and recreation business.

My fellow students on the course were quite a mixed bunch – an ex-footballer, long-distance runner, skier, ex-servicemen etc – and, in terms of age, were mainly in their late 20s or 30s – at 19, I was the baby of the group! What's more, unlike some college prospectuses I've seen, the Premier Training course really delivered what it promised and, as a result, I am now working for North Wiltshire District Council, my base being a sport and leisure centre in the town of Corsham. The centre aims to meet the needs of the whole community (whether a school, sporting club, family or individual) and has facilities for swimming, badminton, weight training, squash, judo, five-a-side football, canoeing and tabletennis, in addition to aerobics, circuit training, a fully equipped gym and a sauna.

My challenge, as a fitness consultant and trainer, is to devise personalised programmes that will make an individual feel healthier, fitter and, as a bonus, give them a surge in self-esteem. For many clients this may involve losing some weight or, in contrast, I may be dealing with someone who needs to develop body strength again after an accident or illness. With a new client I will start by assessing their current level of fitness. This involves checking blood pressure, amount of body fat, flexibility and lung efficiency. I will also take the opportunity to find out more about their current lifestyle and, by careful questioning, their personal aims and objectives.

From this I will formulate a fitness programme that is tailored to their individual requirements and, whenever possible, be on hand to give advice and encouragement. However, I always stress to clients that a fitness evaluation is not a once-only exercise because, as likely as not, there will be a need to be re-evaluated as needs and fitness levels can change significantly. As I say in all my publicity, 'anybody with any body can benefit from my services'.

The variety, of course, makes it such an interesting area of work and I feel, looking back, that I have come a long way in a relatively short period. However, anyone aiming to come into this type of job must realise that evening and weekend work is often par for the course. First and foremost we are a service industry and therefore have to be open when the public wants us. Although our users may one day demand 24-hour access (not yet, thankfully!), we are already part way down that road by being open for over 15 hours a day.

**And the future?** That's easy to answer. My long-term aim is to have my own sports clinic.

## ☐ SPORTS THERAPY

Since the first Olympic Games in Ancient Greece, sports players have, in pursuit of their sport, become sidelined by injury. These days, thanks to a far greater understanding of anatomy, physiology and kinesiology (the study of the mechanics of body movement), many sports players take a positive approach to injury prevention by understanding the nature and cause of typical sports injuries. But injuries will always occur – from broken bones to cartilage problems and strained or torn ligaments – which, in turn, ensures a steady flow of work for people trained in sports therapy and rehabilitation.

Physiotherapy, as a profession, deals not just with sports injuries but covers a wide range of injuries and conditions. This is reflected in the content of university and hospital-based school of physiotherapy courses that, at first degree or diploma level, do not specialise in sports injuries. Once qualified as a physiotherapist, you can then focus on sports injuries and may wish to undertake further training (for example, on a specialist therapy course that teaches skills like sports massage and the treatment of sport-related soft tissue injuries). Students taking a Sports Science degree will, in some cases, also become knowledgeable about sporting injuries and may be able to take a vocational qualification alongside their degree, depending on the institution. However, like physiotherapists, they may also consider it worthwhile taking more vocationally focused training before trying to work professionally as a sports therapist.

In recent years many cities have acquired privately owned sports clinics and, in addition, there are opportunities to work freelance in the sports field. While it is true that professional sports like football, cricket and rugby all value highly the skills of sports therapists, only a relatively small number of physiotherapists are employed full time by clubs and, in the main, they conduct their sports work on a private basis alongside more mainstream physiotherapy work.

### Related careers
Osteopathy as a career has developed steadily in the past few years. An osteopath treats ailments through the manipulation of bones and joints and, in terms of the National Health Service, is not officially recognised; treatment, therefore, is available through private clinics rather than NHS hospitals.

## ☐ SPORTS PRODUCT DESIGN

Twenty years ago the average gym used rudimentary equipment like a sit-up bench and free-standing weights. Today, growing emphasis on health and fitness in many people's lives has been mirrored by more scientifically designed training programmes with equipment that has become increasingly sophisticated. Using the latest engineering design techniques, a new generation of multigym machinery provides exercise programmes that can be tailored to the needs of individuals, able-bodied or disabled, and can provide detailed monitoring of the human body's response to exercise.

Away from the health and fitness suite, too, sports equipment designers have been equally busy. Be it a golf club, motor bike leathers or a rugby scrummaging machine, all have undergone redesign in the light of new knowledge about how the body works and new developments in materials technology. Opportunities exist for suitably qualified designers on an increasing basis, both in Britain and overseas, who have the right blend of engineering know-how, creative flair and understanding of biomechanics.

### Related careers
Sports clothing is a multimillion pound industry which increasingly influences mainstream fashion and provides employment for a large number of people. Within the retail sector there are opportunities to market and sell specialist sports goods such as clothing, food and drink and exercise equipment.

# ☐ GROUNDSMANSHIP

In our fast-changing world there are comparatively few jobs that you can say, with absolute conviction, will still require a high degree of human know-how in a hundred years' time. But no computer yet invented can get near matching a good groundsman's knowledge of local weather, turf, soil, fertilisers, grass seed, rollers, mowing techniques, sprinkler systems, line marking... The list is endless.

While a few UCAS institutions offer courses at degree or HND level in Golf Course Management, many older groundsmen have worked their way up from the bottom, learning on the job as they went along, and benefiting from the experience of wise 'old hands'. As a junior parks worker, for example, the job will primarily revolve around routine maintenance, removing fallen leaves, cutting hedges and, in the summer, cutting grass. Do not expect to become a top-notch groundsman overnight – five years is usually considered the minimum – and to get there, you will need to convince the Institute of Groundsmanship (the profession's national association with members in a wide range of sports, including football, cricket, rugby, bowls, tennis, golf, hockey and horse racing), that you have reached the required level of competence for membership.

Despite the name, there are equal opportunities for women as well as men. One thing that you will need, whether male or female, is an aptitude for working out in the open air which, Britain being Britain, will usually mean that you will get a lot of opportunity to perfect your rainwater removal techniques!

At the very highest level, a golf greenkeeper attached to a championship course can attract the sort of salary that most other groundsmen can only dream about. However, all groundsmen share the possible displeasure of players if the playing surface leads to an unpredictable bounce or is too muddy or the grass is deemed to be too long. These are occupational hazards and, in the long term, even themselves out when a groundsman has the satisfaction of saving an event from postponement due to skill and hard work.

UCAS courses are available at Cannington College (University of the West of England), University of Central Lancashire, Harper Adams College and Writtle College in Essex.

### Related careers
There are opportunities for undersoil heating specialists and most new stadiums include such facilities in their specifications. Watering systems, too, have become much more sophisticated with the advent of computerised programs and there are opportunities to work in sales and marketing in these fields.

# ☐ OUTDOOR PURSUITS/ACTIVITY HOLIDAYS

Whether it is abseiling, snow boarding, caving, climbing, raft racing, canoeing or a host of other sports, an increasing number of people want to use their leisure time engaged in sporting activity rather than just sitting on a beach doing nothing more strenuous than turning the pages of a book. To cater for this tremendous interest, a large service industry has sprung up offering tuition and instruction, whether on a daily basis or as part of a holiday package, to people of all ages. This, in turn, has created a buoyant employment market for qualified instructors who have proven technical competence in a sport, enjoy working with people and are looking for a non 9 to 5 routine.

All bona fide outdoor pursuits companies will be ultra safety conscious and will, as a matter of principle, only employ suitably qualified individuals as activity instructors. Often, this will mean holding qualifications from the national governing body for your sport (eg in canoeing, the British Canoe Union) although a recent initiative, by the Sport and Recreation Industry Training Organisation, has led to the introduction of national vocational qualifications (NVQs). To succeed as an instructor you must be able to develop an empathy for the needs of your clients and, if teaching novices, introduce the sport in a way that will want them to come back again and develop their skills.

In general, most outdoor pursuits work is seasonal – for example, a contract may run from April to September. This suits many young people who, free of commitments, can use the other six months to travel or concentrate on developing prowess in their chosen sport.

### Related careers

Most larger outdoor pursuit centres offer a range of work opportunities which do not require practical sporting ability. For example, a residential centre will need catering skills, stores and domestic assistants, drivers and, at night, security guards. In addition, there are opportunities to work for camping and outdoor clothing and equipment manufacturers in sales and marketing.

**CASE STUDY**

PETER THOMPSON – TRAINING MANAGER, PGL TRAVEL

With more than 40 years' experience, PGL is a main player in outdoor activity holidays for children. In that time, approximately two million children have sampled one of our holidays. We have people who 20 years ago attended as kids now paying us the ultimate compliment of entrusting their own children to us. Having the trust of parents is absolutely vital, because without that it would be impossible to operate and all the activities that we offer, whether in Britain or at one of our European centres, are underpinned by a stringent regard for the safety and well-being of our young clients. Like a stick of seaside rock, the word 'safety' runs through everything we do.

We annually recruit over 2000 staff to work at our centres in Britain, France and Spain and, as Training Manager, I am right at the heart of the process to ensure that we maintain our reputation for highly trained and motivated members of staff who, importantly, like being in the company of children.

Given the size of our organisation, we can offer a wide range of opportunities and because we tend to employ for a season at a time this particularly appeals to many young adults who do not wish to commit themselves to a company for life. This seems very much in tune with the employment market of the 21st century when, as likely as not, working 25 years in the same salaried job will become the exception, and to prosper you will need to be adaptable, resourceful and willing to update your skills – as well as learn totally new ones.

Throughout the season we have vacancies for instructors with

48

qualifications in a wide range of activities – for example, sailing, canoeing, rafting, surfing, pony trekking, archery, fencing, abseiling, mountain biking and climbing; in addition, during July and August we also have a limited number of vacancies for leaders who can offer skills in arts and crafts, drama and video film-making. In support services, there are opportunities to join us as a driver, cook, domestic or stores assistant or night security guard.

Our philosophy is fun and adventure within a framework of safety, and to work as a specific activity instructor it is absolutely vital to have reached a high level of competence in your chosen activity. For the vast majority, this will mean they have achieved recognition by the national governing body for their particular sport. So, for example, our water sports instructors will usually have already gained qualifications from bodies like the British Canoe Union or the Royal Yachting Association. However, they will be willing to continually update their skills, both in relation to their technical knowledge and ability to empathise with our clients.

Put simply, all the technical skill in the world is useless if you lack the communication skills and outgoing character to work with a bunch of lively children. Not surprisingly, some of our most successful seasonal workers have gone on to fulfilling teaching careers and, no doubt, their schools are benefiting from the skills they developed here. For others, the special relation between staff and children that we foster becomes addictive and they stay with us; indeed, most of our centre managers and senior members of staff at head office are fellow sports enthusiasts who have been promoted from within the organisation.

# ☐ RECREATION MANAGEMENT

Sport and leisure centres are now a familiar part of our lives, but this was not always the case; in fact, as recently as 25 years ago sports centres were very few and far between and, in terms of facilities, were often what we would today think of as spartan. Since then, lifestyle changes and the increased emphasis on health and fitness has transformed facilities in Britain. All sport and leisure facilities, whether a small gym or a nationally advertised theme park, need professional management skills. This has led to the creation of a new profession – recreation management.

Traditionally, opportunities had existed for coming in at a junior level (say, as a school leaver in a swimming baths). By taking various qualifications and attending various courses over a number of years, it was theoretically possible to progress through to a supervisory role. This certainly rang true when swimming pools were built and run as separate ventures but, increasingly, swimming is just one of a number of activities offered within a large sport and leisure centre. Due to the increased scale of operation, managing such a complex multiactivity centre calls for a range of expertise that, increasingly, is filled by people who have higher education qualifications. There are now many colleges and universities that offer leisure management courses and, in addition to named degrees and HNDs, opportunities exist to take leisure management options as part of other sport and business management courses.

It is also possible to enter leisure and recreation management from a non-sport first degree. After graduating, no matter what the degree subject, it is possible to study for a Diploma in Management Studies (DMS) or take, at university, a postgraduate course in leisure and recreation management.

### Related careers
Theme parks are a phenomenon of the last two decades, and in the next century they will offer a huge number of work opportunities. There are also opportunities in the leisure industry to manage the use of heritage sites and facilities within National Parks.

# ☐ SPORTS JOURNALISM

An enduring tradition of British journalism is that sports coverage appears at the back of the newspaper. In recent years the column space on most national and regional newspapers has increased and, at the same time, the range of sports covered has widened. In addition, one of the biggest growth areas in magazine publishing has been in sport and leisure and your local newsagent will stock several weekly and monthly sports-oriented titles on their shelves. All this may give the impression that openings for sports journalists are plentiful. The truth is that while opportunities do exist for talented and trained individuals, as in most media-related work, there are always many more hopefuls than positions available.

Traditionally, many journalists have started work on their local paper and, these days, there are added opportunities through the advent of free newspapers, as well as the longer-established regional dailies, weeklies and evening papers. At trainee reporter level, you are likely to work as a generalist and, in time honoured fashion, gain experience by covering local court stories, weddings and festivals. To maximise your chances of success, the National Council for the

Training of Journalists (NCTJ) recommends that would-be journalists take a one-year pre-entry college course. Offered by less than a dozen colleges and universities in Britain, competition for places is very keen and applications should be made as early as possible (see Useful Addresses on page 89).

It is also possible to enter journalism at postgraduate level, following completion of one of the handful of courses validated by British colleges and universities. Examples include University of Wales Institute Cardiff, Strathclyde University and the University of Central Lancashire.

Finally, although some football clubs (mainly in the Premiership) now produce their own colour magazines for sale in newsagents, we have some way to go to match the intensity of football reporting in, say, Italy where newspapers exist that are devoted to nothing but football!

### Related careers
Radio and television journalism are a big lure to many young people but, again, the huge number of applicants means disappointment for the majority of hopefuls.

## CASE STUDY

### KEITH HAYES – FOOTBALL FANZINE EDITOR

Like may supporters I got into this form of journalism because I felt frustrated at the lack of information that my club saw fit to provide for fans. Whether we are talking about the Premiership or the three divisions of the football league, club directors invariably seem content to keep supporters in the dark, hence the creation in the 1980s of football fanzines, written by supporters for supporters.

Although the first examples were very cheap and cheerful and, like myself, most editors have full-time non-journalism jobs (in my case, I am a policeman), some fanzines – for example, *When Saturday Comes* – have since gained widespread recognition and national sales. Just about every professional football club now has at least one fanzine and, on an increasing basis, fanzine creators are also setting up Internet websites.

Realistically, 'don't give up the day job' is the message for most fanzine editors or contributors. But, for a small number of individuals, it has proved an entry into sports journalism as a career.

# ☐ SPORTS PHOTOGRAPHY

Although many sporting events can now be viewed first hand by satellite or terrestrial TV, newspaper sports picture editors still want to cover the story the next day with good action photographs, hence the continual need for photographers who have the twin virtues of alertness (look away, and that vital wicket might be taken) and technical competence. To which should be added resilience and, if working in Britain, an ability to withstand the notorious fickleness of the weather and despite, say, driving rain still come up with good photographs of the action. An experienced photographer comments:

*'In club rugby you are allowed to follow the play up and down the pitch and many good photographs can come from a set piece like the line out. Whereas at a football match you are a static observer parked to one side of the goal posts. It is certainly true that you are close to the action (literally, one photographer was knocked out cold by a wayward shot at a Wembly match!) but, in fact, it is hard to see the match as a spectator would because you are totally focused on coming away with the best shots.'*

Although sports magazines are one of the biggest growth areas in publishing, even combined with newspaper work the number of openings is strictly limited. The majority of photographers are self-employed and make a living by selling their photographs either to picture agencies or direct to newspapers and magazines.

Some established photographers are entirely self-taught but, increasingly, entrants to the profession have qualifications gained at college. In addition to degree and higher national diploma courses, for which applications should be made through UCAS, there are numerous part-time and evening courses run by local education authorities. The National Council for the Training of Journalists, through Stradbroke College in Sheffield, runs an official pre-entry course for press photography (ie it does not just cover sport).

### *Related careers*
The scientific study of sport and human performance needs trained technicians to use high-speed cine cameras and video to analyse techniques (say, of an athlete, diver or rower). Other possibilities include working for a photographic agency or within a photographic library or archive that contains sporting material.

# ☐ SPORTS DEVELOPMENT OFFICER

Many sports development programmes centre on improving sporting activities for young people. The Youth Sports Trust, based at Loughborough University, has the impressive aim of setting up a sports activity programme within every British primary school by the year 2000 and, to implement it, has already trained 10,000 primary teachers and donated equipment to individual schools. The main objective of many sports development projects is to widen participation in sport among youngsters and, in doing so, ensure that the next generation of adults realises the benefits of regular exercise and healthy lifestyles. Although many schemes have been funded in deprived urban areas, there are also initiatives in more rural areas and projects that are aimed at adults, including senior citizens, as well as young people and the disabled. Through sports development programmes, schools and sports centres have been able to offer a wide range of sports including wheelchair basketball, athletics, powerlifting and swimming. While the paralympics, attracting worldwide media coverage, has done much to publicise the achievements of disabled sports people.

At local authority level, the director of leisure will have a sizeable budget and will, within constraints, aim to meet the needs of the local community. However, it is inevitable that many worthy projects would not see the light of day without help from the Sports Council via the National Lottery Sports Fund and, in human terms, the determination of people on the ground, including many in a voluntary capacity, to make things happen. The planning, development and managing of sporting development activity is, like leisure and recreation management, a phenomenon of the past 20 years, and provides employment for a growing number of graduates with sport and leisure related qualifications.

On the management side, good organisational skills and an ability to work within a budget are more important than a high level of sporting ability; however, for development work that involves coaching many officers are sports players themselves and therefore can communicate their enthusiasm for sporting activity to clients.

### *Related careers*
The Sports Council, funded by the government, has a main office in London as well as regional offices and offers employment opportunities ranging from processing grant applications to advising

sports clubs on how to help disabled members of the public gain access to sporting facilities. Most football clubs and a growing number of rugby clubs now employ community development officers to foster good relations and nurture young players.

# ☐ SPORTS BUSINESS WORLD

Every reader of this book will be aware that professional sport has an extremely high profile in both broadcast and print media. In other words, it is big business and therefore the ideal vehicle for many sponsors and advertisers to market their services to the general public. Players and clubs, too, are well aware of the financial pull of sport and, to maximise revenue earning opportunities, increasingly employ professional advisers. There is no one preferred background to enter this kind of work, although many people have backgrounds in accountancy, the legal profession, marketing or public relations.

Although a lot of media coverage has been extended to football agents, this is just one area of activity and, to all intents and purposes, is controlled by just a handful of people in Britain. Far more people work as commercial managers and the fruits of their labour can be seen by the proliferation of advertising hoardings and sponsor logos that are now part and parcel of most professional sporting occasions. Hospitality packages, usually for corporate clients, are the norm for big sporting fixtures. This may include a champagne reception at a nearby hotel, transport to the match and, once there, a pre-match meal in the company of a famous ex-player. For the ex-player, of course, this is an ideal opportunity to earn income on the back of a high-profile sporting career that might only have lasted ten years.

### *Related careers*
Sports equipment endorsements by famous players, whether from the world of basketball, football or athletics, is something that we are all familiar with and, from a business viewpoint, generates large amounts of money, as does the sale of replica kit by football clubs.

Working for a travel agency that specialises in sporting-themed holidays is another option, for instance to watch England play cricket test matches in the West Indies or, for a Premiership football club, to organise the travel arrangements for a big match in Europe.

## JOHN PARKER – REGISTERED MARKETING CONSULTANT

Good marketing is vital if you don't want your product or services to remain a well-kept secret. This might seem a case of stating the obvious but, believe me, some sports goods companies and leisure organisations still get it wrong. For example, you might produce the best saddles and related equine products in the country, but as a company you still need to market you wares effectively. How would I advise such a company...?

My first step would be to work out exactly where their market lies and what products suit that sector of the market. I would look at all their existing promotional literature and, if necessary, revamp it. As a next step I would suggest that they start a website to give themselves a worldwide client base.

A lot of my work is about getting a 'feel' for a market and, in this case, it is obvious that large agricultural and countryside events like the Bath and West Show, the East of England Show and the Badminton Horse Trials are ideal places to display products and meet a lot of potential customers.

To maximise the company's effectiveness at such events, I would also give advice on their exhibition stand and, as part of my marketing mix, arrange training in presentation skills for every member of staff representing the company at such events.

In my experience, many people working in sports business and marketing have marketing or business administration qualifications. This is my background and it gives me the confidence to work for a wide range of clients, which means that I am far from limited to seeking work in the sport and leisure field.

# STUDENT PROFILES

## ☐ ROSIE

'I started getting into hockey and athletics at my secondary school in Norfolk. Later, at sixth-form college in Cambridge, I benefited from having a qualified hockey coach on the PE staff and an inspirational teacher in the art department. Although I am only 24 I have had several stops and starts in my studies and, along the way, attended several different colleges.

'Start number one was an art foundation course in Norwich, in my native Norfolk, which was followed – at the risk of sounding like a character in a Roald Dahl story – by a stint working in a chocolate factory. Start number two, a year later, saw me embarking on a teaching qualification (BA with qualified teacher status) at a college in Yorkshire. I left at the end of the first year and went back to Norwich. Although I was initially unemployed I kept myself fit through running and biking and enrolled on a six-month course to gain an initial qualification in outdoor pursuits.

'It was a very practical course, which suited me down to the ground, with opportunities to pursue my interest in canoeing, climbing, walking and sailing. At the back of my mind, however, was the thought that my A-level studies were being wasted and, after a session with a careers officer, I decided to apply through UCAS for a degree course that combined sport and art. Liverpool Hope University College, the newest of Liverpool's three universities, seemed to have the right mix of facilities and, two years into my degree, I have no regrets in coming up to Merseyside.

'Like most sports studies courses in Britain, theory plays a large part and, like it or not, that is a fact of life. To anyone shaping up to make an application – it is a popular subject, so that will mean literally thousands of young people – I would say don't be lulled into thinking that studying sports at university is just about playing your favourite sport. Of course, proven prowess in one or more sports will certainly help your cause, but the majority of admissions tutors will be keen to assess whether you can hack things like the study of body movement (biomechanics) and, to boot, understand the theories that underpin the psychology of competitive sport.

'To supplement my grant, I work most holidays and some weekends in an outdoor pursuits centre in North Wales. It is challenging work, as most of the centre's clients are youngsters who have been excluded from mainstream schooling due to behavioural problems. In a very "unschooly" atmosphere the youngsters can learn climbing, canoeing and orienteering skills, courtesy of qualified instructors, and work through the problems that got them excluded in the first place. Back at university, I am kept busy by being the secretary of the mountaineering club and, as a confirmed non-couch potato, I have also joined the university's kick boxing club. Which is quite enough exercise, believe me, as I need to keep back energy for my art studies and essay writing.

'Looking into the future, I don't see myself in a desk-bound managerial job. I'd like to create a lifestyle that harmoniously combines my interest in art and sport.'

# ☐ KAREN

'I am a third-year student on the BSc Exercise and Sports Science at Exeter University, sited at the former St Luke's College of Education, specialising in Sports Coaching Science leading to a career in sports development.

'My school days were spent in the London area where I took A-levels in PE, Business Studies and German. The PE A-level is not, as some people seem to think, about how many press-ups you can do in a minute. In fact it is a very demanding mix of anatomy, physiology, the history of PE and psychology plus, for good measure, a practical assessment of your proficiency in a chosen sport. The list of approved sports is quite comprehensive but is dominated by traditional sports (swimming, hockey, athletics, etc) rather than so-called radical sports like snowboarding or paragliding. If an applicant does not have PE or Sports Studies A-level, it would make good sense to do a science GNVQ or one or more science A-levels (say, biology) as sports science does entail laboratory sessions.

'My favourite sports are swimming and hockey. I am lucky in that I can earn extra money because I am a qualified swimming teacher. In addition, I have taken courses in tennis and hockey coaching. St Luke's is very helpful in this respect, offering various coaching qualifications which, as a student, you can take alongside your degree and at preferential enrolment rates. I am in the university hockey team and this takes us all over the southwest to play other sides. If we finish in the top two of our regional league, which we usually do, we will then progress to a national competition to find the best university hockey side in Britain. However, I also have to find time in my week to coach youngsters in the Exeter City swimming club – it's a busy life!

'All of my six UCAS choices were sports related and, rather than apply blind, I visited an Open Day before making a firm decision to apply. The course, which is only two years old, offers three strands, namely, coaching sciences, health and exercise sciences and a non-specialist combination of the two which, for some students, will lead to a teaching career after a Post Graduate Certificate in Education specialising in PE. From what I can gather talking to students at other universities, most higher education sports studies courses are now geared towards sports science, sports development or leisure management. Which makes sense, because this is where most of the work opportunities are now cropping up.

'As students, it is very important for us to be proactive and try to make things happen – in terms of jobs – well before we graduate. This means making use of every contact that you can possibly make, not just in your college or university but with relevant individuals and organisations in the sporting and leisure fields. For example, I have been very active in forging links with Sports Development Officers in the southwest as, given my interest in promoting grass-roots participation in sport, I need to network with people like that.

'It also ties in with my final year dissertation which looks at current initiatives to promote sport to younger age groups. In doing so, I am working closely with the Amateur Swimming Association (ASA) and in particular its junior development programme 'Swim 2000'. In a nutshell, this is about ensuring that junior swimming club members have access to a structured education and development programme, ages 12–16, to maximise their potential and, to be blunt, ensure they are not lost to the sport. At that age, of course, you are very susceptible to peer pressure – going to discos and 6.30am swimming sessions do not mix well! The project revolves around educating swimmers' coaches and parents on the latest thinking on issues like stroke analysis, nutrition and warm-up exercises. Then there's psychology. Having a knowledge of psychology is important when, for example, you are dealing with difficult parents who think they know best on how to turn little Johnny or Amanda into an Olympic Gold Medal swimmer!

'I have taken out student membership of the Institute of Leisure Amenities Management (ILAM), which I believe is a good investment because not only do I receive an informative newsletter (with lots of contact names for networking) but, as a bonus, a circular full of jobs. As I said earlier, most of the job action seems to be very definitely in the sports sciences, sports development and leisure management fields and, as students, we are doing everything possible to hit the ground running when we graduate.'

## ☐ CHRIS

'Looking back, I realise that I was very lucky at both primary and secondary level to have excellent PE teachers. While that is not unusual at secondary level, it certainly was at primary level and I am really indebted to them for arousing my interest in sport. I attended school and sixth-form college in Hereford and took A-levels in English, Psychology and PE. PE was always my main interest and, before applying through UCAS, I researched in some depth a target list of institutions which included Cheltenham and Gloucester College of Higher Education, Exeter University, Leeds Metropolitan University, Loughborough University, University College Chester and University of Wales Institute Cardiff.

When I got to Exeter, in October 1996, I soon realised from talking to fellow students that quite a few of us shared the experience of having done sports studies or PE A-level. Although the majority of my year had studied A-levels, other students had come in through GNVQ, diplomas or (in the case of mature students) Access courses. The first year is very much a foundation course that introduces you to the many facets of the subject and, should anyone arrive harbouring misconceptions, they will realise from week one that the course is not about endless games of sport.

Although Exercise and Sports Science as a named degree course has only be going at Exeter University for two years, the name of St

Luke's is known throughout Britain as a centre for training PE teachers and, along the way, has turned out a lot of very good sportsmen and women. The strong campus identity is reinforced by the fact that many students wear training tops with St Luke's insignia and a lot of social life – surprise, surprise – revolves around our campus bar and common room, including a television set with a screen nearly as wide as the football goalposts at Wembly!

'My main sport is hockey, for which I am a qualified coach, although like most students on the course I enjoy a wide range of sport and outdoor pursuits. This is not the sort of course that appeals to couch potatoes or, for that matter, people who want to sit reading books in the library all day. But, having said that, sporting ability by itself is definitely not enough. You must be able to communicate confidently through the medium of the written word and, for good measure, have enough science to get you through modules like biomechanics. During the first year I lived on campus in a hall of residence, which was an interesting experience; now, as a second year, I share a house off campus with a bunch of other students.

'My future plans are very fluid. On the one hand, I have always had a hankering to join the Marines (which does not have to happen immediately, graduates can enter up to the age of 26), but if the circumstances are right, I might be tempted to continue down a research path, here in Exeter, by doing the university's MSc in Sport and Exercise Psychology. Sports consultancy, very much a vogue career, is something which appeals to me – and about a million other sport science students, too! The realisation that corporate clients are increasingly turning to the sports world for ideas about how best to cement a strong team spirit among members of staff has, for me, been a real eye-opener. This is good news for the growing number of training and development consultancies that have been set up, often involving ex-professional sports people as marketing figureheads, and which, looking ahead, appears to be a job area that will continue to grow.'

## ☐ ANDREW

'My first priority in choosing a degree was to find something that I would find interesting enough to hold my commitment for three years. As a very keen sports player – cricket is my main sport – I decided to look for a college or university that could offer a

combination of sports studies and business management.
Cheltenham and Gloucester College of Higher Education, my local
higher education institution, offered this pairing and, having applied
through UCAS, that's where I am now studying full time as a first-
year degree student.

'My BSc Sports Science (major) and Business Management (minor)
strikes a good balance between developing my interest in sport and
exercise, which is obviously to my liking, but set against a solid
grounding in modern business and administration techniques. This
will, I hope, make me an attractive proposition to future employers,
come summer 2000, and my graduation.

'My dad, who is a PE teacher and keen amateur cricketer, planted
the initial seeds of my interest and, from an early age, I always
seemed to be playing one sport or another. My main sport is now
very much cricket and as a wicket keeper I have played for
Gloucestershire under 19s. I mentioned this on my personal
statement when I applied through UCAS and as a result I gained a
two-point exemption on my offer from Cheltenham and Gloucester
College of Higher Education.

'Like most sports science courses that I have read about, our first
year is comprised of a series of core modules on subjects like
biomechanics, anatomy, physiology and psychology of sport. Our
laboratory time is approximately two hours every three weeks, we
have about 12 hours a week of lectures and seminars, and the rest of
our time is self-directed study.

'My original plan was to take a year off after A-levels and do some
travelling. I had a contact in Zimbabwe and there was a possibility
that I could go out there and do some cricket coaching, but then the
introduction of tuition fees hit the news and I decided to get in as
soon as possible. I estimate that I have spent about £75 on course
books so far, although I am lucky in that my dad can get me some of
the necessary books and others, in business studies, I have managed
to buy second-hand.

'There is no need to spend a lot of money on sporting equipment
because, to be realistic, the amount of time given over to playing
sport is only a small part of my degree. However, the college has
been helpful because it can supply things like tracksuits and
sweatshirts at prices that are lower than local shops. In terms of

facilities, everything that we need is here and, what's more, kept in very good condition through sponsorship deals with local companies.

'Although I chose to study and live at home many of my fellow students are from other parts of the country. Many of us have found part-time jobs to help our grants go further (in my case, I work about 12 hours a week on the till at a Safeways supermarket) and that, it seems, is the reality of being a student now. Student loans are another reality. I have taken out a student loan, yes, but following advice from my old economics teacher I have invested most of it in a high interest savings account; which, I suppose, is just the sort of thing that the business management part of my course would approve of!'

## ☐ LIZZIE

'I was raised in care of the local authority and attended a number of schools around London and the Home Counties. After school I took a hand glass-blowing apprenticeship. This was quite a novelty, believe me, as the industry was very chauvinistic and it was not easy for me to try to make my way. The company, which specialised in glass bowls for technical and scientific equipment, decided that it would be a good idea to relocate to the southwest, which it did, but it all went pear-shaped for me as I found myself out of a job.

'My involvement with community sports started by helping out as a volunteer on local play schemes and sporting activity events for youngsters in the Yeovil area of Somerset. Funds were tight and to help out I tried my hand at finding companies and individuals who were willing to provide sponsorship to buy things like jerseys and shorts. In doing so I was very aware that my eldest son, who had difficult behaviour, had been helped thanks to the patience and sympathetic ear of the Professional Football Association (PFA) football development officer at our local league club. Seeing this made me want to follow in his footsteps with other children – by harnessing their natural love of sport and, in particular, football. This meant (with guidance from my mentor the PFA development officer) setting out to gain football coaching qualifications awarded by the sport's governing body, the Football Association.

'As you can probably guess, football is not awash with female coaches and, like my former glass-blowing career, I knew that I would have to try doubly hard to convince sceptical lads and their fathers that a woman can coach the sport as well as a man. Anyway, the upshot of this was that I got my feet on the first rung of the coaching ladder by gaining my FA leader's award and the National Coaching Foundation (NCF) award for coaching children, giving first aid etc. Not content to leave it there, I made the decision to push on and try for the best coaching qualifications available.

'When you are unemployed there is a tendency to lose your self-belief and just drift along living life a day at a time. Luckily, I found my way into the local adult education guidance centre and with their encouragement and guidance (thanks, Jean) I started to map out a new future for myself. To maximise my chances of working in the field of sports development I decided, after advice, to enter higher education. No one in my family had ever done this before and, to be honest, I was quite nervous at the prospect. Having two sons, the course would have to be local and, after conducting some research, I discovered that Yeovil College ran an HND in Business Management Leisure, franchised from Bournemouth University and that, even better, this included a sport and leisure option. I applied and, to my great relief, was offered a place.

'The first year of my HND has covered all aspects of business practice, marketing, communications and management of people and health and safety. It will give me a good range of business and coaching skills to offer a future employer. At the same time, liking a challenge, I am part way towards qualifying for a prestigious football coaching qualification, the Football Association Coaching Certificate and NVQ Level 2 Sport and Recreation Coaching Adults and Children, which is recognised by both the Football Association and the Union of European Football Associations (UEFA). This is a very demanding qualification and requires a sound understanding of many different topics, including nutrition, fitness, health and safety, child psychology, working with disabled youngsters, the laws of the game and, last but not least, ethics and sportsmanship.

'At community sport level, which is where I want to operate, the name of the game is "sport for all" and mere involvement, rather than being a star individual performer, is what it is all about. For example, the Foyer project, for which I did some coaching sessions, gave homeless young people in the Yeovil area an opportunity to actively participate in sport. Trying to win over a group of 16–21-year-old men that as a woman I could coach them football skills and then weld them into a team – it was a challenge, believe me! Not surprisingly, they were a bit unsure of me at first (vice versa, to be honest!) but after one session the issue of my gender melted away and it was so gratifying when they started to get a buzz from the idea of forming a team, looking for fixtures, sorting out a pitch and so on.

'When I have completed my HND, I would very much like to work in the field of sports development. As an activity, sport shatters barriers and therefore it can help to heal the sense of exclusion from society which many youngsters feel. It is not glamorous work, but I would much rather use my football coaching skills to help turn youngsters away from possible involvement with crime and drug abuse than do any other job.'

# A–Z OF INSTITUTIONS AND STATISTICAL TABLES

## ☐ USER GUIDE

In this chapter you will find listed all the UCAS institutions that offer courses in sport and leisure. These are listed alphabetically in two tables, starting with leisure, in the same order that they appear in the UCAS *Handbook* for 1999. Each institutional entry panel itemises the number of courses available, degree and/or HND, and provides, for guidance purposes only, minimum entry requirements for a number of pre-higher education qualifications.

## Key

### *A-level/AS-level*
Offers may be expressed in terms of a points total or range of points or grades. Points are calculated as follows:

| Grade | A-level | AS-level |
|-------|---------|----------|
| A | 10 | 5 |
| B | 8 | 4 |
| C | 6 | 3 |
| D | 4 | 2 |
| E | 2 | 1 |

### *Advanced GNVQ*
Offers may be expressed as follows:

P  Pass in AGNVQ required
M  Merit in AGNVQ required
D  Distinction in AGNVQ required

### *Edexcel Foundation (BTEC) National Certificate/Diploma*
Successful completion of a relevant National Certificate/Diploma is assumed. This will sometimes be sufficient for entry (listed as 'N' in the tables), but in other cases applicants will be required to meet certain criteria. Examples include:

| M | Merit grades required: specific number given where appropriate |
|---|---|
| D | Distinction grades required: specific number given where appropriate |
| MO | Grades of merit in all units, or equivalent overall/average |
| DO | Distinctions required in all units |
| M–D | No standard offer, but some merit and distinction grades will be expected |
| HN | Completion of Higher National Diploma Certificate/Diploma |
| $ | Specific units must be included |
| Ind | Considered on an individual basis – refer to institution |
| X | Not normally sufficient for entry |

### *Scottish Qualifications Authority (SQA)*
Offers based on Highers will cover the range of grades A–C.

**Note that where an institution has more than one course in sport or leisure the quoted requirement is derived from averaging out requirements for individual courses.** Before making a formal application, it is vital to contact institutions for more detailed information on entry requirements to particular courses. To help you do this speedily, this chapter provides full postal addresses, telephone and fax numbers and, where available, e-mail and Internet (www) addresses.

# INSTITUTIONS OFFERING COURSES IN LEISURE

UCAS code: A30
**University of Abertay Dundee**
Bell Street, Dundee DD1 1HG
tel: 01382 308080; fax: 01382 308877
e-mail: iro@abertay-dundee.ac.uk
www: http://www.tay.ac.uk/

|  | HND | Degree |
|---|---|---|
| No of courses |  | 3 |
| A-level score |  | 12 |
| GNVQ |  |  |
| SQA grades |  | BBBC |
| BTEC |  |  |

UCAS code: A55
**Amersham & Wycombe College**
Stanley Hill, Amersham HP7 9HN
tel: 01494 735500
fax: 01494 735566

|  | HND | Degree |
|---|---|---|
| No of courses | 1 |  |
| A-level score |  |  |
| GNVQ | P |  |
| SQA grades |  |  |
| BTEC | N |  |

UCAS code: A60
**Anglia Polytechnic University**
East Road, Cambridge CB1 1PT
tel: 01223 363271; fax: 01223 576156
e-mail: degaalap@bridge.anglia.ac.uk
www: http://www.anglia.ac.uk/

|  | HND | Degree |
|---|---|---|
| No of courses | 1 | 4 |
| A-level score | 8 | 12 |
| GNVQ | P | M |
| SQA grades | CCCC | BCCC |
| BTEC | 2M | 4M |

UCAS code: B06
**University of Wales Bangor**
Bangor LL57 2DG
tel: 01248 382017; fax: 01248 370451
e-mail: Ainsley@bangor.ac.uk
www: http://www.bangor.ac.uk/

|  | HND | Degree |
|---|---|---|
| No of courses |  | 4 |
| A-level score |  | 13 |
| GNVQ |  | M |
| SQA grades |  | BBBC |
| BTEC |  | 4M |

UCAS code: B13
**Barnsley College**
Old Mill Lane Site, Church Street
Barnsley S70 2AX
tel: 01226 730191/216229; fax: 01226 216613
e-mail: L.Kirk@barnsley.ac.uk
www: http://www.barnsley.ac.uk/he

|  | HND | Degree |
|---|---|---|
| No of courses | 3 |  |
| A-level score | 3 |  |
| GNVQ | P |  |
| SQA grades |  |  |
| BTEC | 2M |  |

UCAS code: B26
**Bell College of Technology**
Almada Street, Hamilton, Lanarkshire ML3 0JB
tel: 01698 283100; fax: 01698 282131
e-mail: registry@bell.ac.uk

|  | HND | Degree |
|---|---|---|
| No of courses | 1 | 2 |
| A-level score | 4 | 6 |
| GNVQ | P |  |
| SQA grades | CC | CCC |
| BTEC | N |  |

UCAS code: B32
**The University of Birmingham**
Edgbaston, Birmingham B15 2TT
tel: 0121 414 3697; fax: 0121 414 3850
e-mail: prospectus@birmingham.ac.uk
www: http://www.birmingham.ac.uk

|  | HND | Degree |
|---|---|---|
| No of courses |  | 1 |
| A-level score |  | 24 |
| GNVQ |  |  |
| SQA grades |  |  |
| BTEC |  |  |

UCAS code: B35
**Birmingham College of Food, Tourism & Creative Studies**
Summer Row, Birmingham B3 1JB
tel: 0121 604 1040; fax: 0121 200 1376
e-mail: admissions@bcftcs.ac.uk
www: http://www.bcftcs.ac.uk/

|  | HND | Degree |
|---|---|---|
| No of courses | 4 | 8 |
| A-level score | 4 | 12 |
| GNVQ | P | M |
| SQA grades |  |  |
| BTEC | 4M | MO |

UCAS code: B40
**Blackburn College,** Faculty of Creative Arts
Feilden Street, Blackburn BB2 1LH
tel: 01254 55144; fax: 01254 682700

|  | HND | Degree |
|---|---|---|
| No of courses | 1 | |
| A-level score | 2 | |
| GNVQ | P | |
| SQA grades | | |
| BTEC | N | |

UCAS code: B41
**Blackpool & The Fylde College**
Ashfield Road, Bispham, Blackpool FY2 0HB
tel: 01253 352352; fax: 01253 356127
www: http://www.blackpool.ac.uk/

|  | HND | Degree |
|---|---|---|
| No of courses | 4 | 4 |
| A-level score | 3 | 4 |
| GNVQ | P | M |
| SQA grades | | |
| BTEC | N | HN+4 |

UCAS code: B44
**Bolton Institute of Higher Education**
Deane Road, Bolton BL3 5AB
tel: 01204 528851; fax: 01204 399074
e-mail: enquiries@bolton.ac.uk.
www: http://www.mmm.co.uk/bi/index.html

|  | HND | Degree |
|---|---|---|
| No of courses | | 42 |
| A-level score | | 10 |
| GNVQ | | M |
| SQA grades | | BBCC |
| BTEC | | MO |

UCAS code: B50
**Bournemouth University**
Studland House, 12 Christchurch Road
Bournemouth, BH1 3NA
tel: 01202 524111; fax: 01202 503869
e-mail: postmaster@bournemouth.ac.uk
www: http://www.bournemouth.ac.uk/

|  | HND | Degree |
|---|---|---|
| No of courses | 2 | 4 |
| A-level score | 6 | 13 |
| GNVQ | P | M |
| SQA grades | BCC | BBCC |
| BTEC | MO | MO |

UCAS code: B60
**Bradford & Ilkley Community College**
Great Horton Road, Bradford BD7 1AY
tel: 01274 753026; fax: 01274 741060
e-mail: admissions@bilk.ac.uk
www: http://www.bilk.ac.uk/

|  | HND | Degree |
|---|---|---|
| No of courses | 3 | 3 |
| A-level score | 4 | 8 |
| GNVQ | P | M |
| SQA grades | | |
| BTEC | 3M | M+D |

UCAS code: B72
**University of Brighton**
Mithras House, Lewes Road, Brighton BN2 4AT
tel: 01273 600900; fax: 01273 642825
e-mail: admissions@bton.ac.uk.
www: http://www.brighton.ac.uk/

|  | HND | Degree |
|---|---|---|
| No of courses | 1 | 7 |
| A-level score | 2 | 13 |
| GNVQ | P | M |
| SQA grades | CC | BBBCC |
| BTEC | N | 3M+3 |

UCAS code: B80
**University of the West of England, Bristol**
Frenchay Campus, Coldharbour Lane
Bristol BS16 1QY
tel: 0117 965 6261; fax: 0117 976 3804
e-mail: admissions@uwe.ac.uk.
www: http://www.uwe.ac.uk

|  | HND | Degree |
|---|---|---|
| No of courses | | 2 |
| A-level score | | 16 |
| GNVQ | | M |
| SQA grades | | BBCC |
| BTEC | | MO+ |

UCAS code: B84
**Brunel University,** Uxbridge UB8 3PH
tel: 01895 274000; fax: 01895 203167
e-mail: courses@brunel.ac.uk
www: http://www.brunel.ac.uk/home.html

|  | HND | Degree |
|---|---|---|
| No of courses | | 4 |
| A-level score | | 19 |
| GNVQ | | M |
| SQA grades | | BBCC |
| BTEC | | 2M+3 |

UCAS code: B90
**The University of Buckingham**
Hunter Street, Buckingham MK18 1EG
tel: 01280 814080; fax: 01280 824081
e-mail: admissions@buck.ac.uk
www: http://www.buck.ac.uk

|  | HND | Degree |
|---|---|---|
| No of courses | | 2 |
| A-level score | | 13 |
| GNVQ | | M |
| SQA grades | | BCCC |
| BTEC | | 3M+2 |

UCAS code: B94
**Buckinghamshire Chilterns University College**
Queen Alexandra Rd, High Wycombe HP11 2JZ
tel: 01494 522141; fax: 01494 524392
www: http://www.buckscol.ac.uk/bchome.html

|  | HND | Degree |
|---|---|---|
| No of courses | 2 | 48 |
| A-level score | 8 | 8 |
| GNVQ | M | M |
| SQA grades | CCCC | CCCC |
| BTEC | MO | MO |

UCAS code: C10
**Canterbury Christ Church College of Higher Education,** Canterbury CT1 1QU
tel: 01227 767700; fax: 01227 470442
e-mail: admissions@cant.ac.uk.
www: http://www.cant.ac.uk/

|  | HND | Degree |
|---|---|---|
| No of courses | 1 | 49 |
| A-level score | 4 | 11 |
| GNVQ | P | M |
| SQA grades |  |  |
| BTEC | N | MO |

UCAS code: C20
**University of Wales Institute Cardiff**
PO Box 377, Llandaff Centre
Western Avenue, Cardiff CF5 2SG
tel: 01222 506044/47; fax: 01222 506956
e-mail: admissions@uwic.ac.uk
www: http://www.uwic.ac.uk/

|  | HND | Degree |
|---|---|---|
| No of courses | 3 | 18 |
| A-level score | 5 | 13 |
| GNVQ | M | M |
| SQA grades | CC | CCC |
| BTEC | MO | MO |

UCAS code: C25
**University of Central England in Birmingham**
Perry Barr, Birmingham B42 2SU
tel: 0121 331 5595; fax: 0121 331 6358
www: http://www.uce.ac.uk/

|  | HND | Degree |
|---|---|---|
| No of courses |  | 1 |
| A-level score |  | 12 |
| GNVQ |  | M |
| SQA grades |  | CCC |
| BTEC |  | MO |

UCAS code: C30
**University of Central Lancashire,** Preston PR1 2HE
tel: 01772 892400; fax: 01772 892935
e-mail: c.enquiries@uclan.ac.uk
www: http://www.uclan.ac.uk/

|  | HND | Degree |
|---|---|---|
| No of courses | 7 | 7 |
| A-level score | 4 | 14 |
| GNVQ | P | M |
| SQA grades | CC | BBBC |
| BTEC | N | MO |

UCAS code: C50
**Cheltenham & Gloucester College of Higher Education**
The Park, PO Box 220, Cheltenham GL50 2QF
tel: 01242 532824/6; fax: 01242 256759
e-mail: admissions@chelt.ac.uk
www: http://www.chelt.ac.uk/

|  | HND | Degree |
|---|---|---|
| No of courses | 2 | 167 |
| A-level score | 2 | 11 |
| GNVQ | P | M |
| SQA grades |  | CCCC |
| BTEC | N | MO+ |

UCAS code: C55
**University College Chester**
Cheyney Road, Chester CH1 4BJ
tel: 01244 375444; fax: 01244 373379
www: http://www.chester.ac.uk/

|  | HND | Degree |
|---|---|---|
| No of courses |  | 1 |
| A-level score |  | 10 |
| GNVQ |  | M |
| SQA grades |  | CCC |
| BTEC |  | MO |

UCAS code: C63
**City of Bristol College**
Hartcliffe Centre, Bishport Avenue
Hartcliffe, Bristol BS13 ORJ
tel: 0117 904 5000; fax: 0117 904 5050

|  | HND | Degree |
|---|---|---|
| No of courses | 2 |  |
| A-level score |  |  |
| GNVQ |  |  |
| SQA grades |  |  |
| BTEC |  |  |

UCAS code: C66
**City College Manchester**
PO Box 40, Manchester M23 0GN
tel: 0161 957 1790; fax: 0161 945 3854
e-mail: admissions@manchester-city-coll.ac.uk
www: http://www.manchester-city-coll.ac.uk/

|  | HND | Degree |
|---|---|---|
| No of courses | 1 |  |
| A-level score | 2 |  |
| GNVQ | M |  |
| SQA grades |  |  |
| BTEC | MO |  |

UCAS code: C75
**Colchester Institute**
Sheepen Road, Colchester CO3 3LD
tel: 01206 718000; fax: 01206 763041

|  | HND | Degree |
|---|---|---|
| No of courses | 2 | 20 |
| A-level score | 4 | 8 |
| GNVQ | P | P |
| SQA grades |  |  |
| BTEC | 3M |  |

UCAS code: C78
**Cornwall College with Duchy College**
Redruth, Cornwall TR15 3RD
tel: 01209 712911; fax: 01209 718802
e-mail: enquiries@corncoll.ac.uk

|  | HND | Degree |
|---|---|---|
| No of courses | 4 |  |
| A-level score | 4 |  |
| GNVQ | P |  |
| SQA grades |  |  |
| BTEC | 2M |  |

69

UCAS code: C85
**Coventry University**
Priory Street, Coventry CV1 5FB
tel: 01203 631313; fax: 01203 838793
www: http://www.coventry.ac.uk/

|  | HND | Degree |
|---|---|---|
| No of courses |  | 4 |
| A-level score |  | 13 |
| GNVQ |  | M |
| SQA grades |  | CCC |
| BTEC |  | 4M |

UCAS code: C92
**Croydon College**
Fairfield, Croydon CR9 1DX
tel: 0181 760 5892; fax: 0181 760 5880
e-mail: info@croydon.ac.uk
www: http://www.croydon.ac.uk/

|  | HND | Degree |
|---|---|---|
| No of courses | 2 |  |
| A-level score | 2 |  |
| GNVQ | P |  |
| SQA grades |  |  |
| BTEC | N |  |

UCAS code: C95
**Cumbria College of Art & Design**
Brampton Road, Carlisle CA3 9AY
tel: 01228 400300; fax: 01228 514491

|  | HND | Degree |
|---|---|---|
| No of courses | 1 | 1 |
| A-level score | 2 | 4 |
| GNVQ | M | M |
| SQA grades | B | BB |
| BTEC | N | N |

UCAS code: D26
**De Montfort University**
The Gateway, Leicester LE1 9BH
tel: 0116 255 1551; fax: 0116 257 7515
www: http://www.dmu.ac.uk/

|  | HND | Degree |
|---|---|---|
| No of courses | 2 | 12 |
| A-level score | 4 | 10 |
| GNVQ | P | M |
| SQA grades | BB | BBCC |
| BTEC | N | DO |

UCAS code: D39
**University of Derby**
Kedleston Road, Derby DE22 1GB
tel: 01332 622289; fax: 01332 622754
e-mail: m.a.crowther@derby.ac.uk
www: http://www.derby.ac.uk/

|  | HND | Degree |
|---|---|---|
| No of courses | 1 | 2 |
| A-level score | 4 | 14 |
| GNVQ | M | D |
| SQA grades | CCC | BBCC |
| BTEC | MO | HN |

UCAS code: D52
**Doncaster College**
Waterdale, Doncaster DN1 3EX
tel: 01302 553718; fax: 01302 553559
www: http://www.don.ac.uk/

|  | HND | Degree |
|---|---|---|
| No of courses | 1 |  |
| A-level score | 6 |  |
| GNVQ | P |  |
| SQA grades |  |  |
| BTEC | 4M |  |

UCAS code: D65
**University of Dundee**
Dundee DD1 4HN
tel: 01382 344160; fax: 01382 221554
e-mail: srs@dundee.ac.uk
www: http://www.dundee.ac.uk/

|  | HND | Degree |
|---|---|---|
| No of courses |  | 1 |
| A-level score |  | 12 |
| GNVQ |  | M |
| SQA grades |  | BBC |
| BTEC |  | 6M |

UCAS code: E42
**Edge Hill University College**
St Helens Road, Ormskirk L39 4QP
tel: 01695 584312; fax: 01695 579997
e-mail: ibisona@admin.ehche.ac.uk
www: http://www.ehche.ac.uk/

|  | HND | Degree |
|---|---|---|
| No of courses |  | 1 |
| A-level score |  | 12 |
| GNVQ |  | M |
| SQA grades |  | BBCC |
| BTEC |  | 3M+3 |

UCAS code: F66
**Farnborough College of Technology**
Boundary Road, Farnborough GU14 6SB
tel: 01252 407028; fax: 01252 407041
e-mail: admissions@farn-ct.ac.uk
www: http://www.farn-ct.ac.uk/

|  | HND | Degree |
|---|---|---|
| No of courses | 4 | 1 |
| A-level score | 6 | 12 |
| GNVQ | P | M |
| SQA grades |  |  |
| BTEC |  |  |

UCAS code: G14
**University of Glamorgan**
Pontypridd CF37 1DL
tel: 01443 482684; fax: 01443 482014
www: http://www.glam.ac.uk/home.html

|  | HND | Degree |
|---|---|---|
| No of courses | 1 | 4 |
| A-level score | 6 | 13 |
| GNVQ | P | M |
| SQA grades |  |  |
| BTEC | N | MO+ |

UCAS code: G42
**Glasgow Caledonian University**
Cowcaddens Road, Glasgow G4 0BA
tel: 0141 331 3334; fax: 0141 331 3449
e-mail: d.black@gcal.ac.uk
www: http://www.gcal.ac.uk/

|  | HND | Degree |
|---|---|---|
| No of courses | 1 | 4 |
| A-level score | 4 | 12 |
| GNVQ |  |  |
| SQA grades | CC | BBCC |
| BTEC |  |  |

UCAS code: G45
**Gloucestershire College of Arts & Technology**
Brunswick Campus, Brunswick Road
Gloucester GL1 1HU
tel: 01452 426557; fax: 01452 426531

|  | HND | Degree |
|---|---|---|
| No of courses | 2 |  |
| A-level score | 2 |  |
| GNVQ | P |  |
| SQA grades |  |  |
| BTEC | N |  |

UCAS code: G70
**University of Greenwich**
Avery Hill Campus, Mansion Site
Bexley Road, Eltham SE9 2PQ
tel: 0181 331 8044; fax: 0181 331 9856
e-mail: p.fisher@greenwich.ac.uk
www: http://www.gre.ac.uk/

|  | HND | Degree |
|---|---|---|
| No of courses | 3 | 4 |
| A-level score | 6 | 14 |
| GNVQ |  | M |
| SQA grades | CC | CCC |
| BTEC | MO |  |

UCAS code: H16
**Herefordshire College of Technology**
Folly Lane, Hereford HR1 1LS
tel: 01432 352235; fax: 01432 353449
www: http://www.herefordshire.com/hct/

|  | HND | Degree |
|---|---|---|
| No of courses | 2 | 3 |
| A-level score | 2 | 8 |
| GNVQ | M | M |
| SQA grades | CC | CC |
| BTEC |  |  |

UCAS code: H36
**University of Hertfordshire**
Mercer Building, College Lane, Hatfield AL10 9AB
tel: 01707 284800; fax: 01707 284870
www: http://www.herts.ac.uk/

|  | HND | Degree |
|---|---|---|
| No of courses | 2 | 1 |
| A-level score | 5 | 18 |
| GNVQ | M | M |
| SQA grades | CCCC | BBBB |
| BTEC | MO | DO |

UCAS code: H60
**The University of Huddersfield**
Queensgate, Huddersfield HD1 3DH
tel: 01484 422288; fax: 01484 516151
e-mail: prospectus@hud.ac.uk
www: http://www.hud.ac.uk/

|  | HND | Degree |
|---|---|---|
| No of courses | 1 | 3 |
| A-level score | 2 | 9 |
| GNVQ | P | P |
| SQA grades | CC | BBBC |
| BTEC | N |  |

UCAS code: L24
**Leeds, Trinity & All Saints University College**
Brownberrie Lane, Horsforth
Leeds LS18 5HD
tel: 0113 283 7123; fax: 0113 283 7200
www: http://www.tasc.ac.uk/

|  | HND | Degree |
|---|---|---|
| No of courses |  | 2 |
| A-level score |  | 18 |
| GNVQ |  |  |
| SQA grades |  | AABBB |
| BTEC |  | MO+ |

UCAS code: L27
**Leeds Metropolitan University**
Calverley Street, Leeds LS1 3HE
tel: 0113 283 3113; fax: 0113 283 3114
e-mail: course-enquiries@lmu.ac.uk
www: http://www.lmu.ac.uk/

|  | HND | Degree |
|---|---|---|
| No of courses | 3 | 6 |
| A-level score | 7 | 15 |
| GNVQ | M | D |
| SQA grades | BBC | BBBB |
| BTEC | MO | MO+ |

UCAS code: L36
**Leicester South Fields College**
Aylestone Road, Leicester LE2 7LW
tel: 0116 224 2200; fax: 0116 224 2190

|  | HND | Degree |
|---|---|---|
| No of courses | 2 |  |
| A-level score | 2 |  |
| GNVQ | P |  |
| SQA grades |  |  |
| BTEC |  |  |

UCAS code: L39
**University of Lincolnshire & Humberside**
Milner Hall, Cottingham Road, Hull HU6 7RT
tel: 01482 440550; fax: 01482 463310
e-mail: marketing@ac.humber.uk
www: http://www.ulh.ac.uk/

|  | HND | Degree |
|---|---|---|
| No of courses | 4 | 21 |
| A-level score | 4 | 15 |
| GNVQ | P | M |
| SQA grades | CC | BBBCC |
| BTEC | M | 1M+4 |

**UCAS code: L43**
**Liverpool Community College**
Hope Street Centre, Hope Street, Liverpool L1 9EB
tel: 0151 252 3000; fax: 0151 707 2597

|  | HND | Degree |
|---|---|---|
| No of courses | 1 |  |
| A-level score |  |  |
| GNVQ |  |  |
| SQA grades |  |  |
| BTEC |  |  |

**UCAS code: L46**
**Liverpool Hope University College**
PO Box 6, Stand Park Road, Liverpool L16 9JD
tel: 0151 291 3000; fax: 0151 291 3048
www: http://www.livhope.ac.uk/

|  | HND | Degree |
|---|---|---|
| No of courses |  | 14 |
| A-level score |  | 11 |
| GNVQ |  | P |
| SQA grades |  |  |
| BTEC |  | 8M |

**UCAS code: L51**
**Liverpool John Moores University**
Roscoe Court, 4 Rodney Street, Liverpool L1 2TZ
tel: 0151 231 5090/5091; fax: 0151 231 3194
e-mail: recruitment@livjm.ac.uk
www: http://www.livjm.ac.uk/

|  | HND | Degree |
|---|---|---|
| No of courses |  | 2 |
| A-level score |  | 16 |
| GNVQ |  |  |
| SQA grades |  |  |
| BTEC |  |  |

**UCAS code: L53**
**Llandrillo College (North Wales)**
Llandudno Road, Colwyn Bay LL28 4HZ
tel: 01492 546666; fax: 01492 543052
e-mail: admissions@llandrillo.ac.uk

|  | HND | Degree |
|---|---|---|
| No of courses | 3 | 1 |
| A-level score |  |  |
| GNVQ |  |  |
| SQA grades |  |  |
| BTEC |  | HN |

**UCAS code: L65**
**The London Institute**
65 Davies Street, London W1Y 2DA
tel: 0171 514 6000; fax: 0171 514 6131
e-mail: marcom@linst.ac.uk
www: http://www.lond-inst.ac.uk/

|  | HND | Degree |
|---|---|---|
| No of courses | 1 | 1 |
| A-level score |  |  |
| GNVQ |  |  |
| SQA grades |  |  |
| BTEC |  |  |

**UCAS code: L79**
**Loughborough University**
Ashby Road, Loughborough LE11 3TU
tel: 01509 263171; fax: 01509 223905
e-mail: w.j.clarke@lboro.ac.uk
www: http://www.lboro.ac.uk/

|  | HND | Degree |
|---|---|---|
| No of courses |  | 2 |
| A-level score |  | 25 |
| GNVQ |  | D |
| SQA grades |  |  |
| BTEC |  | 4D |

**UCAS code: L93**
**University of Luton,** Park Square, Luton LU1 3JU
tel: 01582 489286; fax: 01582 489323
e-mail: pat.herber@luton.ac.uk.
www: http://www.luton.ac.uk/

|  | HND | Degree |
|---|---|---|
| No of courses | 2 | 5 |
| A-level score | 8 | 14 |
| GNVQ | M | D |
| SQA grades | BBCC | BBCC |
| BTEC | M | 5M |

**UCAS code: M20**
**The University of Manchester**
Manchester M13 9PL
tel: 0161 275 2077; fax: 0161 275 2407
e-mail: ug.admissions@man.ac.uk
www: http://www.man.ac.uk/

|  | HND | Degree |
|---|---|---|
| No of courses |  | 1 |
| A-level score |  | 20 |
| GNVQ |  | D |
| SQA grades |  | ABBBB |
| BTEC |  | MO+ |

**UCAS code: M40**
**The Manchester Metropolitan University**
All Saints, Manchester M15 6BH
tel: 0161 247 2966; fax: 0161 247 6311
e-mail: prospectus@mmu.ac.uk
www: http://www.mmu.ac.uk/

|  | HND | Degree |
|---|---|---|
| No of courses | 5 | 6 |
| A-level score | 6 | 12 |
| GNVQ | M | D |
| SQA grades | C | BBC |
| BTEC |  | M+D |

**UCAS code: M77**
**Mid-Cheshire College**
Hartford Campus, Northwich CW8 1LJ
tel: 01606 74444; fax: 01606 75101
www: http://www.midchesh.u-net.com/

|  | HND | Degree |
|---|---|---|
| No of courses | 2 |  |
| A-level score | 2 |  |
| GNVQ |  |  |
| SQA grades |  |  |
| BTEC | 3M |  |

UCAS code: M80
**Middlesex University**
White Hart Lane, London N17 8HR
tel: 0181 362 5898; fax: 0181 362 5649
e-mail: admissions@mdx.ac.uk
www: http://www.mdx.ac.uk/

|  | HND | Degree |
| --- | --- | --- |
| No of courses | 2 | 1 |
| A-level score | 2 | 10 |
| GNVQ | P | M |
| SQA grades | | |
| BTEC | N | 5M |

UCAS code: M90
**Moray House Institute of Education**
Holyrood Road, Edinburgh EH8 8AQ
tel: 0131 556 8455; fax: 0131 557 3458
www: http://www.mhie.ac.uk/

|  | HND | Degree |
| --- | --- | --- |
| No of courses | | 1 |
| A-level score | | 16 |
| GNVQ | | |
| SQA grades | | BBCC |
| BTEC | | |

UCAS code: N07
**Napier University**
219 Colinton Road, Edinburgh EH14 1DJ
tel: 0131 455 4330; fax: 0131 455 4666
e-mail: info@napier.ac.uk
www: http://www.napier.ac.uk/

|  | HND | Degree |
| --- | --- | --- |
| No of courses | | 11 |
| A-level score | | 11 |
| GNVQ | | M |
| SQA grades | | BBCC |
| BTEC | | |

UCAS code: N23
**Newcastle College**, Ryehill Campus, Scotswood
Road, Newcastle upon Tyne NE4 7SA
tel: 0191 200 4110; fax: 0191 272 4297
e-mail: sdoughty@ncl-coll.ac.uk
www: http://www.ncl-coll.ac.uk/

|  | HND | Degree |
| --- | --- | --- |
| No of courses | 2 | |
| A-level score | | |
| GNVQ | | |
| SQA grades | | |
| BTEC | | |

UCAS code: N41
**Northbrook College Sussex**, Littlehampton Road,
Goring by Sea, Worthing BN12 6NU
tel: 01903 606060; fax: 01903 606007
e-mail: admissions@NBCOL.ac.uk
www: http://www.NBCOL.ac.uk

|  | HND | Degree |
| --- | --- | --- |
| No of courses | 1 | |
| A-level score | 6 | |
| GNVQ | | |
| SQA grades | | |
| BTEC | 3M | |

UCAS code: N49
**Nescot**, Reigate Road, Ewell, Epsom KT17 3DS
tel: 0181 394 1731; fax: 0181 394 3030
e-mail: lclewlow@nescot.ac.uk
www: http://www.nescot.ac.uk/

|  | HND | Degree |
| --- | --- | --- |
| No of courses | 2 | |
| A-level score | 3 | |
| GNVQ | P | |
| SQA grades | | |
| BTEC | 6M | |

UCAS code: N58
**North East Worcestershire College**
Blackwood Road, Bromsgrove, Worcs B90 1PQ
tel: 01527 570020; fax: 01527 572901

|  | HND | Degree |
| --- | --- | --- |
| No of courses | 3 | |
| A-level score | | |
| GNVQ | | |
| SQA grades | | |
| BTEC | | |

UCAS code: N63
**University of North London**
166–220 Holloway Road, London N7 8DB
tel: 0171 753 5066; fax: 0171 753 5075
e-mail: admissions@unl.ac.uk
www: http://www.unl.ac.uk/

|  | HND | Degree |
| --- | --- | --- |
| No of courses | 3 | 14 |
| A-level score | 7 | 13 |
| GNVQ | | M |
| SQA grades | CCC | CCCC |
| BTEC | 10M | |

UCAS code: N77
**University of Northumbria at Newcastle**
Ellison Building, Ellison Place
Newcastle upon Tyne NE1 8ST
tel: 0191 227 4064; fax: 0191 227 3009
e-mail: rg.admissions@unn.ac.uk
www: http://www.unn.ac.uk/

|  | HND | Degree |
| --- | --- | --- |
| No of courses | | 3 |
| A-level score | | 15 |
| GNVQ | | D |
| SQA grades | | BBBCC |
| BTEC | | MO |

UCAS code: N82
**Norwich City College**
Ipswich Road, Norwich NR2 2LJ
tel: 01603 773136; fax: 01603 773334
e-mail: registry@ccn.ac.uk
www: http://www.ccn.ac.uk/

|  | HND | Degree |
| --- | --- | --- |
| No of courses | 3 | 3 |
| A-level score | 2 | 6 |
| GNVQ | P | P |
| SQA grades | | |
| BTEC | N | HN |

UCAS code: N91
**The Nottingham Trent University**
Burton Street, Nottingham NG1 4BU
tel: 0115 941 8418; fax: 0115 948 6063
www: http://www.ntu.ac.uk/

|               | HND | Degree |
| ------------- | --- | ------ |
| No of courses | 4   | 2      |
| A-level score | 8   | 12     |
| GNVQ          | M   | M      |
| SQA grades    | C   |        |
| BTEC          | MO  | M+D    |

UCAS code: O66
**Oxford Brookes University**
Gipsy Lane Campus, Headington, Oxford OX3 0BP
tel: 01865 483040; fax: 01865 483983
www: http://www.brookes.ac.uk/

|               | HND | Degree |
| ------------- | --- | ------ |
| No of courses |     | 119    |
| A-level score |     | 12     |
| GNVQ          |     | M      |
| SQA grades    |     |        |
| BTEC          |     |        |

UCAS code: P20
**University of Paisley**
High Street, Paisley PA1 2BE
tel: 0141 848 3859; fax: 0141 848 3623
e-mail: fras-ap0@paisley.ac.uk
www: http://www.paisley.ac.uk/

|               | HND | Degree |
| ------------- | --- | ------ |
| No of courses |     | 1      |
| A-level score |     | 12     |
| GNVQ          |     |        |
| SQA grades    |     | BBC    |
| BTEC          |     |        |

UCAS code: P60
**University of Plymouth**
Drake Circus, Plymouth PL4 8AA
tel: 01752 232135; fax: 01752 232179
e-mail: c.todd@plymouth.ac.uk
www: http://www.plym.ac.uk/

|               | HND | Degree |
| ------------- | --- | ------ |
| No of courses | 8   | 5      |
| A-level score | 4   | 11     |
| GNVQ          | P   | M      |
| SQA grades    |     | BBC    |
| BTEC          | MO  | 4M     |

UCAS code: P80
**University of Portsmouth,** University House,
Winston Churchill Avenue, Portsmouth PO1 2UP
tel: 01705 876543; fax: 01705 843082
e-mail: admissions@reg.port.ac.uk
www: http://www.port.ac.uk/

|               | HND | Degree |
| ------------- | --- | ------ |
| No of courses |     | 3      |
| A-level score |     | 12     |
| GNVQ          |     | M      |
| SQA grades    |     | CCCC   |
| BTEC          |     | 5M+1   |

UCAS code: Q25
**Queen Margaret College, Edinburgh**
Clerwood Terrace, Edinburgh EH12 8TS
tel: 0131 317 3247; fax: 0131 317 3248
e-mail: admissions@mail.qmced.ac.uk
www: http://www.qmced.ac.uk/

|               | HND | Degree |
| ------------- | --- | ------ |
| No of courses |     | 3      |
| A-level score |     | 9      |
| GNVQ          |     | M      |
| SQA grades    |     | BBC    |
| BTEC          |     | M+D    |

UCAS code: R10
**Reading College & School of Arts & Design**
King's Road, Reading RG1 4HJ
tel: 0118 967 5555; fax: 0118 967 5001

|               | HND | Degree |
| ------------- | --- | ------ |
| No of courses | 1   |        |
| A-level score |     |        |
| GNVQ          |     |        |
| SQA grades    |     |        |
| BTEC          |     |        |

UCAS code: R24
**University College of Ripon & York St John**
Lord Mayor's Walk, York YO3 7EX
tel: 01904 616850; fax: 01904 616921
e-mail: l.waghorn@ucrysj.ac.uk
www: http://www.ucrysj.ac.uk/

|               | HND | Degree |
| ------------- | --- | ------ |
| No of courses |     | 1      |
| A-level score |     | 14     |
| GNVQ          |     | M      |
| SQA grades    |     | BBBC   |
| BTEC          |     | M      |

UCAS code: R36
**The Robert Gordon University**
Schoolhill, Aberdeen AB10 1FR
tel: 01224 262105; fax: 01224 262133
e-mail: j.youngson@rgu.ac.uk
www: http://www.rgu.ac.uk/

|               | HND | Degree |
| ------------- | --- | ------ |
| No of courses | 1   | 2      |
| A-level score | 4   | 7      |
| GNVQ          |     |        |
| SQA grades    | BC  | BBC    |
| BTEC          | N   | N      |

UCAS code: R48
**Roehampton Institute London**
Roehampton Lane, London SW15 5PU
tel: 0181 392 3000; fax: 0181 392 3220
e-mail: admissions@roehampton.ac.uk
www: http://www.roehampton.ac.uk/

|               | HND | Degree |
| ------------- | --- | ------ |
| No of courses |     | 28     |
| A-level score |     | 12     |
| GNVQ          |     | M      |
| SQA grades    |     | BBB    |
| BTEC          |     | 2M+2   |

UCAS code: S01
**Scottish Agricultural College**
Auchincruive, Ayr KA6 5HW
tel: 01292 525350; fax: 01292 525349
e-mail: etsu@au.sac.ac.uk
www: http://www.sac.ac.uk/

|              | HND | Degree |
| ------------ | --- | ------ |
| No of courses | 2   | 1      |
| A-level score | 2   | 12     |
| GNVQ         | P   | M      |
| SQA grades   | CC  | BCC    |
| BTEC         | N   |        |

UCAS code: S03
**The University of Salford**
Salford M5 4WT
tel: 0161 295 5641/5509; fax: 0161 745 3126
e-mail: a.l.farrell@university-management.salford.ac.uk
www: http://www.salford.ac.uk/homepage.html

|              | HND | Degree |
| ------------ | --- | ------ |
| No of courses | 4   | 4      |
| A-level score | 4   | 11     |
| GNVQ         | P   | D      |
| SQA grades   | CC  | BBB    |
| BTEC         | 5M  | M/D    |

UCAS code: S10
**University College Scarborough**
Filey Road, Scarborough YO11 3AZ
tel: 01723 362392; fax: 01723 370815
e-mail: registry@ucscarb.ac.uk
www: http://www.ucscarb.ac.uk/

|              | HND | Degree |
| ------------ | --- | ------ |
| No of courses |     | 2      |
| A-level score |     | 8      |
| GNVQ         |     | P      |
| SQA grades   |     |        |
| BTEC         |     |        |

UCAS code: S21
**Sheffield Hallam University**
Surrey Building, Sheffield S1 1WB
tel: 0114 253 3490; fax: 0114 253 4023
e-mail: c.arnold@shu.ac.uk
www: http://www.shu.ac.uk/

|              | HND | Degree |
| ------------ | --- | ------ |
| No of courses | 3   | 6      |
| A-level score | 4   | 15     |
| GNVQ         | P   | M      |
| SQA grades   |     | CCCC   |
| BTEC         | 4M  | 8M+2   |

UCAS code: S22
**Sheffield College**
PO Box 345, Sheffield S2 2YY
tel: 0114 260 3007; fax: 0114 260 2301

|              | HND  | Degree |
| ------------ | ---- | ------ |
| No of courses | 1    |        |
| A-level score |      |        |
| GNVQ         |      |        |
| SQA grades   |      |        |
| BTEC         | 3M+2 |        |

UCAS code: S23
**Shrewsbury College of Arts & Technology**
London Road, Shrewsbury SY2 7PR
tel: 01743 342342; fax: 01743 241684
e-mail: mail@s-cat.ac.uk

|              | HND | Degree |
| ------------ | --- | ------ |
| No of courses | 2   |        |
| A-level score | 2   |        |
| GNVQ         | P   |        |
| SQA grades   |     |        |
| BTEC         |     |        |

UCAS code: S24
**University College of St Martin, Lancaster & Cumbria,** Bowerham Road, Lancaster LA1 3JD
tel: 01524 384444; fax: 01524 384567
e-mail: admissions@ucsm.ac.uk
www: http://www.ucsm.ac.uk/

|              | HND | Degree |
| ------------ | --- | ------ |
| No of courses |     | 3      |
| A-level score |     | 11     |
| GNVQ         |     | P      |
| SQA grades   |     | BBCC   |
| BTEC         |     |        |

UCAS code: S26
**Solihull College**
Blossomfield Road, Solihull B91 1SB
tel: 0121 678 7001/2; fax: 0121 678 7200
e-mail: enquiries@staff.solihull.ac.uk
www: http://www.solihull.ac.uk/

|              | HND | Degree |
| ------------ | --- | ------ |
| No of courses | 2   | 2      |
| A-level score | 2   |        |
| GNVQ         | P   |        |
| SQA grades   |     |        |
| BTEC         | N   | HN     |

UCAS code: S28
**Somerset College of Arts & Technology**
Wellington Road, Taunton TA1 5AX
tel: 01823 366366; fax: 01823 355418
www: http://www.zynet.co.uk/scat1/

|              | HND | Degree |
| ------------ | --- | ------ |
| No of courses | 2   |        |
| A-level score |     |        |
| GNVQ         |     |        |
| SQA grades   |     |        |
| BTEC         |     |        |

UCAS code: S30
**Southampton Institute**
East Park Terrace, Southampton SO14 0YN
tel: 01703 319039; fax: 01703 334161
e-mail: MS@Solent.ac.uk
www: http://www.solent.ac.uk/

|              | HND  | Degree |
| ------------ | ---- | ------ |
| No of courses | 4    | 2      |
| A-level score | 5    | 7      |
| GNVQ         | P    | M      |
| SQA grades   | CCCC | CCCC   |
| BTEC         | N    | MO     |

UCAS code: S33
**South Bank University**
103 Borough Road, London SE1 0AA
tel: 0171 815 8158; fax: 0171 815 8273
e-mail: enrol@sbu.ac.uk
www: http://www.sbu.ac.uk/

|  | HND | Degree |
|---|---|---|
| No of courses |  | 29 |
| A-level score |  | 12 |
| GNVQ |  | M |
| SQA grades |  |  |
| BTEC |  | 4M+2 |

UCAS code: S38
**Southwark College,** Surrey Docks Centre,
Drummond Road, London SE16 4EE
tel: 0171 815 1600; fax: 0171 815 1525
e-mail: ucas@southwark.ac.uk
www: www.southwark.ac.uk

|  | HND | Degree |
|---|---|---|
| No of courses | 1 |  |
| A-level score | 2 |  |
| GNVQ |  |  |
| SQA grades |  |  |
| BTEC |  |  |

UCAS code: S51
**St Helens College**
Brook Street, St Helens, Merseyside WA10 1PZ
tel: 01744 623338; fax: 01744 623421
www: http://www.sthelens.mernet.org.uk/

|  | HND | Degree |
|---|---|---|
| No of courses | 1 |  |
| A-level score | 2 |  |
| GNVQ | P |  |
| SQA grades |  |  |
| BTEC | N |  |

UCAS code: S59
**The University College of St Mark & St John**
Derriford Road, Plymouth PL19 9AL
tel: 01752 636827; fax: 01752 636849
www: http://194.80.168.100/

|  | HND | Degree |
|---|---|---|
| No of courses |  | 14 |
|  |  |  |
| A-level score |  | 9 |
| GNVQ |  | M |
| SQA grades |  | CCCC |
| BTEC |  | MO |

UCAS code: S72
**Staffordshire University**
College Road, Stoke-on-Trent ST4 2DE
tel: 01782 292752; fax: 01782 745422
e-mail: admissions@staffs.ac.uk
www: http://www.staffs.ac.uk/

|  | HND | Degree |
|---|---|---|
| No of courses |  | 7 |
| A-level score |  | 15 |
| GNVQ |  | M |
| SQA grades |  | BBB |
| BTEC |  | 2M+4 |

UCAS code: S76
**Stockport College of Further & Higher Education**
Wellington Road South, Stockport SK1 3UQ
tel: 0161 958 3416; fax: 0161 958 3305
www: http://www.stockport.ac.uk/

|  | HND | Degree |
|---|---|---|
| No of courses | 2 |  |
| A-level score | 2 |  |
| GNVQ | P |  |
| SQA grades |  |  |
| BTEC | N |  |

UCAS code: S78
**The University of Strathclyde**
McCance Building, 16 Richmond Street
Glasgow G1 1XQ
tel: 0141 548 2814; fax: 0141 552 7362
e-mail: j.foulds@mis.strath.ac.uk
www: http://www.strath.ac.uk/Campus/prospect/info/i

|  | HND | Degree |
|---|---|---|
| No of courses |  | 1 |
| A-level score |  | 18 |
| GNVQ |  |  |
| SQA grades |  | BBBCC |
| BTEC |  |  |

UCAS code: S81
**University College Suffolk**
Rope Walk, Ipswich IP4 1LT
tel: 01473 255885; fax: 01473 230054
www: http://www.suffolk.ac.uk/

|  | HND | Degree |
|---|---|---|
| No of courses | 3 | 4 |
| A-level score | 2 | 5 |
| GNVQ | P | P |
| SQA grades |  |  |
| BTEC | N | N |

UCAS code: S84
**University of Sunderland**
St Mary's Building, Chester Road
Sunderland SR1 3SD
tel: 0191 515 3000; fax: 0191 515 3805
e-mail: student-helpline@sunderland.ac.uk
www: http://www.sunderland.ac.uk/

|  | HND | Degree |
|---|---|---|
| No of courses |  | 5 |
| A-level score |  | 14 |
| GNVQ |  | M |
| SQA grades |  | BBBCC |
| BTEC |  | 6M |

UCAS code: S87
**The University of Surrey,** Guildford GU2 5XH
tel: 01483 300800; fax: 01483 300803
www: http://www.surrey.ac.uk/

|  | HND | Degree |
|---|---|---|
| No of courses |  | 2 |
| A-level score |  | 18 |
| GNVQ |  |  |
| SQA grades |  | BBBB |
| BTEC |  | MO+ |

UCAS code: S96
**Swansea Institute of Higher Education**
Mount Pleasant, Swansea SA1 6ED
tel: 01792 481000; fax: 01792 481263
e-mail: enquiry@sihe.ac.uk
www: http://www.sihe.ac.uk/home.html

|  | HND | Degree |
|---|---|---|
| No of courses |  | 4 |
| A-level score |  | 5 |
| GNVQ |  | P |
| SQA grades |  | CCCC |
| BTEC |  | N |

UCAS code: T20
**University of Teesside**
Borough Road, Middlesbrough TS1 3BA
tel: 01642 218121; fax: 01642 384201
e-mail: H.Cummins@tees.ac.uk
www: http://www@tees.ac.uk/

|  | HND | Degree |
|---|---|---|
| No of courses | 4 | 1 |
| A-level score | 4 | 10 |
| GNVQ | P | M |
| SQA grades |  |  |
| BTEC |  | 3M+3 |

UCAS code: T40
**Thames Valley University**
St Mary's Road, Ealing, London W5 5RF
tel: 0181 579 5000; fax: 0181 231 2900
e-mail: christine.marchant@tvu.ac.uk
www: http://www.tvu.ac.uk/

|  | HND | Degree |
|---|---|---|
| No of courses | 3 | 56 |
| A-level score | 3 | 8 |
| GNVQ | P | M |
| SQA grades | CC | CCC |
| BTEC | N |  |

UCAS code: T80
**Trinity College Carmarthen**
College Road, Carmarthenshire SA31 3EP
tel: 01267 676767; fax: 01267 676766

|  | HND | Degree |
|---|---|---|
| No of courses |  | 11 |
| A-level score |  | 4 |
| GNVQ |  |  |
| SQA grades |  |  |
| BTEC |  |  |

UCAS code: U20
**University of Ulster,** University House, Cromore
Road, Coleraine BT52 1SA
tel: 01265 44141; fax: 01265 324908
e-mail: ja.elliott@ulst.ac.uk
www: http://www.ulst.ac.uk/

|  | HND | Degree |
|---|---|---|
| No of courses |  | 4 |
| A-level score |  | 18 |
| GNVQ |  | M |
| SQA grades |  | ABBB |
| BTEC |  | MO+ |

UCAS code: W17
**University College Warrington**
Padgate Campus, Fearnhead
Warrington WA2 0DB
tel: 01925 494494; fax: 01925 494289
e-mail: registry.he@warr.ac.uk
www: http://www.warr.ac.uk/unicoll.html

|  | HND | Degree |
|---|---|---|
| No of courses | 1 | 4 |
| A-level score | 6 | 10 |
| GNVQ |  |  |
| SQA grades |  |  |
| BTEC |  |  |

UCAS code: W40
**West Herts College, Watford**
Hempstead Road, Watford WD1 3EZ
tel: 01923 812565; fax: 01923 812540

|  | HND | Degree |
|---|---|---|
| No of courses | 4 | 1 |
| A-level score | 2 |  |
| GNVQ |  |  |
| SQA grades |  |  |
| BTEC |  |  |

UCAS code: W50
**University of Westminster**
Metford House, 15–18 Clipstone Street
London W1M 8JS
tel: 0171 911 5000; fax: 0171 911 5858
www: http://www.wmin.ac.uk/

|  | HND | Degree |
|---|---|---|
| No of courses |  | 6 |
| A-level score |  | 7 |
| GNVQ |  | P |
| SQA grades |  | BBB |
| BTEC |  | 3M |

UCAS code: W52
**Westminster College**
Vincent Square, London SW1P 2PD
tel: 0171 828 1222; fax: 0171 931 0347

|  | HND | Degree |
|---|---|---|
| No of courses | 2 | 1 |
| A-level score | 2 |  |
| GNVQ | P |  |
| SQA grades |  |  |
| BTEC | 3M | HN |

UCAS code: W67
**Wigan & Leigh College**
PO Box 53, Parson's Walk, Wigan WN1 1RR
tel: 01942 501528; fax: 01942 501533

|  | HND | Degree |
|---|---|---|
| No of courses | 1 |  |
| A-level score | 8 |  |
| GNVQ |  |  |
| SQA grades |  |  |
| BTEC | N |  |

UCAS code: W73
**Wirral Metropolitan College**
Carlett Park Campus, Eastham, Wirral L62 0AY
tel: 0151 551 7472; fax: 0151 551 7401
e-mail: h.e.enquiries@wmc.ac.uk
www: http://www.wmc.ac.uk

|  | HND | Degree |
|---|---|---|
| No of courses | 3 |  |
| A-level score |  |  |
| GNVQ | M |  |
| SQA grades |  |  |
| BTEC |  |  |

UCAS code: W75
**University of Wolverhampton**
Compton Park Campus
Wolverhampton WV3 9DX
tel: 01902 321000; fax: 01902 323744
e-mail: a.fitzpatrick@wlv.ac.uk
www: http://www.wlv.ac.uk/

|  | HND | Degree |
|---|---|---|
| No of courses | 1 | 3 |
| A-level score | 2 | 15 |
| GNVQ | P | M |
| SQA grades | CCCC | BBBB |
| BTEC | N | 4M |

UCAS code: W80
**University College Worcester**
Henwick Grove, Worcester WR2 6AJ
tel: 01905 855111; fax: 01905 855132
www: http://www.worc.ac.uk/worcs.html

|  | HND | Degree |
|---|---|---|
| No of courses | 1 |  |
| A-level score | 2 |  |
| GNVQ | P |  |
| SQA grades |  |  |
| BTEC | N |  |

UCAS code: W81
**Worcester College of Technology**
Deansway, Worcester WR1 2JF
tel: 01905 725555; fax: 01905 28906

|  | HND | Degree |
|---|---|---|
| No of courses | 1 |  |
| A-level score | 2 |  |
| GNVQ | P |  |
| SQA grades |  |  |
| BTEC | N |  |

UCAS code: W85
**Writtle College**
Writtle, Chelmsford CM1 3RR
tel: 01245 420705; fax: 01245 420456
e-mail: postmaster@writtle.ac.uk
www: http://www.writtle.ac.uk/

|  | HND | Degree |
|---|---|---|
| No of courses | 1 | 1 |
| A-level score | 2 | 10 |
| GNVQ | M | M |
| SQA grades |  |  |
| BTEC | N | MO |

UCAS code: Y80
**Yorkshire Coast College of Further & Higher Education**
Lady Edith's Drive, Scalby Road,
Scarborough YO12 5RN
tel: 01723 372105; fax: 01723 501918
e-mail: admissions@ycoastco.ac.uk
www: http://www.cbconnect.co.uk/ycc.html

|  | HND | Degree |
|---|---|---|
| No of courses | 3 |  |
| A-level score | 2 |  |
| GNVQ | P |  |
| SQA grades |  |  |
| BTEC | N |  |

# INSTITUTIONS OFFERING COURSES IN SPORT

UCAS code: A20
**The University of Aberdeen**
Regent Walk, Aberdeen AB24 8FX
tel: 01224 273504; fax: 01224 272031
e-mail: admoff@admin.abdn.ac.uk
www: http://www.abdn.ac.uk/

|  | HND | Degree |
|---|---|---|
| No of courses |  | 1 |
| A-level score |  | 16 |
| GNVQ |  | M |
| SQA grades |  | BBBC |
| BTEC |  |  |

UCAS code: A60
**Anglia Polytechnic University**
East Road, Cambridge CB1 1PT
tel: 01223 363271; fax: 01223 576156
e-mail: degaalap@bridge.anglia.ac.uk
www: http://www.anglia.ac.uk/

|  | HND | Degree |
|---|---|---|
| No of courses | 1 | 2 |
| A-level score | 4 | 10 |
| GNVQ | P | M |
| SQA grades | CCC | BCCC |
| BTEC | N | 3M |

UCAS code: B06
**University of Wales Bangor**
Bangor LL57 2DG
tel: 01248 382017; fax: 01248 370451
e-mail: Ainsley@bangor.ac.uk
www: http://www.bangor.ac.uk/

|  | HND | Degree |
|---|---|---|
| No of courses |  | 24 |
| A-level score |  | 19 |
| GNVQ |  | M |
| SQA grades |  | BBBB |
| BTEC |  | 5D |

UCAS code: B16
**University of Bath**
Claverton Down, Bath BA2 7AY
tel: 01225 323019; fax: 01225 826366
e-mail: admissions@bath.ac.uk
www: http://www.bath.ac.uk/

|  | HND | Degree |
|---|---|---|
| No of courses |  | 3 |
| A-level score |  | 24 |
| GNVQ |  |  |
| SQA grades |  |  |
| BTEC |  |  |

UCAS code: B26
**Bell College of Technology**
Almada Street, Hamilton,
Lanarkshire ML3 OJB
tel: 01698 283100; fax: 01698 282131
e-mail: registry@bell.ac.uk

|  | HND | Degree |
|---|---|---|
| No of courses | 1 |  |
| A-level score | 4 |  |
| GNVQ | P |  |
| SQA grades | CC |  |
| BTEC | N |  |

UCAS code: B32
**The University of Birmingham**
Edgbaston, Birmingham B15 2TT
tel: 0121 414 3697; fax: 0121 414 3850
e-mail: prospectus@birmingham.ac.uk
www: http://www.birmingham.ac.uk

|  | HND | Degree |
|---|---|---|
| No of courses |  | 2 |
| A-level score |  | 24 |
| GNVQ |  |  |
| SQA grades |  |  |
| BTEC |  |  |

UCAS code: B40
**Blackburn College**
Faculty of Creative Arts, Feilden Street
Blackburn BB2 1LH
tel: 01254 55144; fax: 01254 682700

|  | HND | Degree |
|---|---|---|
| No of courses | 1 |  |
| A-level score |  |  |
| GNVQ |  |  |
| SQA grades |  |  |
| BTEC |  |  |

UCAS code: B41
**Blackpool & The Fylde College**
Ashfield Road, Bispham
Blackpool FY2 0HB
tel: 01253 352352; fax: 01253 356127
www: http://www.blackpool.ac.uk/

|  | HND | Degree |
|---|---|---|
| No of courses | 1 |  |
| A-level score | 2 |  |
| GNVQ | P |  |
| SQA grades |  |  |
| BTEC | N |  |

UCAS code: B44
**Bolton Institute of Higher Education**
Deane Road, Bolton BL3 5AB
tel: 01204 528851; fax: 01204 399074
e-mail: enquiries@bolton.ac.uk.
www: http://www.mmm.co.uk/bi/index.html

|  | HND | Degree |
|---|---|---|
| No of courses |  | 2 |
| A-level score |  | 10 |
| GNVQ |  | M |
| SQA grades |  |  |
| BTEC |  | MO |

UCAS code: B72
**University of Brighton,** Mithras House,
Lewes Road, Brighton BN2 4AT
tel: 01273 600900; fax: 01273 642825
e-mail: admissions@bton.ac.uk.
www: http://www.brighton.ac.uk/

|  | HND | Degree |
|---|---|---|
| No of courses |  | 3 |
| A-level score |  | 16 |
| GNVQ |  | M |
| SQA grades |  | BBBCC |
| BTEC |  | 2M+5 |

UCAS code: B84
**Brunel University,** Uxbridge UB8 3PH
tel: 01895 274000; fax: 01895 203167
e-mail: courses@brunel.ac.uk
www: http://www.brunel.ac.uk/home.html

|  | HND | Degree |
|---|---|---|
| No of courses |  | 4 |
| A-level score |  | 20 |
| GNVQ |  | D |
| SQA grades |  | BBCC |
| BTEC |  | 2M+3 |

UCAS code: B94
**Buckinghamshire Chilterns University College,**
Queen Alexandra Road, High Wycombe HP11 2JZ
tel: 01494 522141; fax: 01494 524392
www: http://www.buckscol.ac.uk/bchome.html

|  | HND | Degree |
|---|---|---|
| No of courses |  | 11 |
| A-level score |  | 8 |
| GNVQ |  | M |
| SQA grades |  | CCCC |
| BTEC |  |  |

UCAS code: C10
**Canterbury Christ Church College of Higher Education,** Canterbury CT1 1QU
tel: 01227 767700; fax: 01227 470442
e-mail: admissions@cant.ac.uk.
www: http://www.cant.ac.uk/

|  | HND | Degree |
|---|---|---|
| No of courses |  | 53 |
| A-level score |  | 11 |
| GNVQ |  | M |
| SQA grades |  |  |
| BTEC |  | MO |

UCAS code: C20
**University of Wales Institute Cardiff**
PO Box 377, Llandaff Centre, Western Avenue,
Cardiff CF5 2SG
tel: 01222 506044/47; fax: 01222 506956
e-mail: admissions@uwic.ac.uk
www: http://www.uwic.ac.uk/

|  | HND | Degree |
|---|---|---|
| No of courses |  | 4 |
| A-level score |  | 16 |
| GNVQ |  | D |
| SQA grades |  | BBB |
| BTEC |  | 4D |

UCAS code: C22
**Carmarthenshire College**
Job's Well Road, Carmarthen SA31 3HY
tel: 01554 748000; fax: 01554 756088
e-mail: eirian.davies@ccta.ac.uk
www: www.ccta.ac.uk

|  | HND | Degree |
|---|---|---|
| No of courses | 1 |  |
| A-level score | 2 |  |
| GNVQ |  |  |
| SQA grades |  |  |
| BTEC |  |  |

UCAS code: C30
**University of Central Lancashire,** Preston PR1 2HE
tel: 01772 892400; fax: 01772 892935
e-mail: c.enquiries@uclan.ac.uk
www: http://www.uclan.ac.uk/

|  | HND | Degree |
|---|---|---|
| No of courses | 1 | 3 |
| A-level score | 4 | 18 |
| GNVQ | P | D |
| SQA grades | CC | BBBB |
| BTEC | N | MO+ |

UCAS code: C50
**Cheltenham & Gloucester College of Higher Education**
The Park, PO Box 220, Cheltenham GL50 2QF
tel: 01242 532824/6; fax: 01242 256759
e-mail: admissions@chelt.ac.uk
www: http://www.chelt.ac.uk/

|  | HND | Degree |
|---|---|---|
| No of courses |  | 74 |
| A-level score |  | 11 |
| GNVQ |  | M |
| SQA grades |  | CCCC |
| BTEC |  | MO+ |

UCAS code: C55
**University College Chester**
Cheyney Road, Chester CH1 4BJ
tel: 01244 375444; fax: 01244 373379
www: http://www.chester.ac.uk/

|  | HND | Degree |
|---|---|---|
| No of courses |  | 40 |
| A-level score |  | 11 |
| GNVQ |  | M |
| SQA grades |  | CCC |
| BTEC |  | MO |

UCAS code: C58
**Chichester Institute of Higher Education**
Bishop Otter College, College Lane
Chichester PO19 4PE
tel: 01243 816000; fax: 01243 816080
e-mail: apps@chihe.ac.uk
www: http://www.chihe.ac.uk/

|  | HND | Degree |
|---|---|---|
| No of courses |  | 2 |
| A-level score |  | 14 |
| GNVQ |  | M |
| SQA grades |  |  |
| BTEC |  |  |

UCAS code: C75
**Colchester Institute**
Sheepen Road, Colchester CO3 3LD
tel: 01206 718000; fax: 01206 763041

|  | HND | Degree |
|---|---|---|
| No of courses |  | 2 |
| A-level score |  | 8 |
| GNVQ |  | M |
| SQA grades |  |  |
| BTEC |  | 6M |

UCAS code: C85
**Coventry University**
Priory Street, Coventry CV1 5FB
tel: 01203 631313; fax: 01203 838793
www: http://www.coventry.ac.uk/

|  | HND | Degree |
|---|---|---|
| No of courses | 1 | 6 |
| A-level score |  | 13 |
| GNVQ |  | M |
| SQA grades |  |  |
| BTEC |  | 6M |

UCAS code: D26
**De Montfort University**
The Gateway, Leicester LE1 9BH
tel: 0116 255 1551; fax: 0116 257 7515
www: http://www.dmu.ac.uk/

|  | HND | Degree |
|---|---|---|
| No of courses | 1 | 40 |
| A-level score | 6 | 13 |
| GNVQ | P | M |
| SQA grades | BB | ABBB |
| BTEC | M | 2M+4 |

UCAS code: D86
**The University of Durham**
Old Shire Hall, Old Elvet, Durham DH1 3HP
tel: 0191 374 2000; fax: 0191 374 7250
www: http://www.dur.ac.uk/

|  | HND | Degree |
|---|---|---|
| No of courses |  | 2 |
| A-level score |  | 17 |
| GNVQ |  |  |
| SQA grades |  | AABBB |
| BTEC |  |  |

UCAS code: E28
**University of East London**
Longbridge Road, Dagenham RM8 2AS
tel: 0181 849 3443; fax: 0181 849 3438
www: http://www.uel.ac.uk/

|  | HND | Degree |
|---|---|---|
| No of courses |  | 1 |
| A-level score |  | 8 |
| GNVQ |  | M |
| SQA grades |  |  |
| BTEC |  | MO |

UCAS code: E42
**Edge Hill University College**
St Helens Road, Ormskirk L39 4QP
tel: 01695 584312; fax: 01695 579997
e-mail: ibisona@admin.ehche.ac.uk
www: http://www.ehche.ac.uk/

|  | HND | Degree |
|---|---|---|
| No of courses |  | 9 |
| A-level score |  | 14 |
| GNVQ |  | P |
| SQA grades |  | BBCC |
| BTEC |  | 3M+3 |

UCAS code: E70
**The University of Essex**
Wivenhoe Park, Colchester CO4 3SQ
tel: 01206 873666; fax: 01206 873423
e-mail: admit@essex.ac.uk
www: http://www.essex.ac.uk/

|  | HND | Degree |
|---|---|---|
| No of courses |  | 4 |
| A-level score |  | 18 |
| GNVQ |  | D |
| SQA grades |  | BBBB |
| BTEC |  | MO+ |

UCAS code: E84
**University of Exeter,** Northcote House,
The Queen's Drive, Exeter EX4 4QJ
tel: 01392 263032; fax: 01392 263857
e-mail: J.C.Clissold@exeter.ac.uk
www: http://www.ex.ac.uk/

|  | HND | Degree |
|---|---|---|
| No of courses | 1 | 1 |
| A-level score | 4 | 20 |
| GNVQ | P | D |
| SQA grades |  |  |
| BTEC |  | MO |

UCAS code: F66
**Farnborough College of Technology**
Boundary Road, Farnborough GU14 6SB
tel: 01252 407028; fax: 01252 407041
e-mail: admissions@farn-ct.ac.uk
www: http://www.farn-ct.ac.uk/

|  | HND | Degree |
|---|---|---|
| No of courses | 2 | 1 |
| A-level score | 5 | 10 |
| GNVQ | P | M |
| SQA grades |  |  |
| BTEC |  |  |

UCAS code: G14
**University of Glamorgan,** Pontypridd CF37 1DL
tel: 01443 482684; fax: 01443 482014
www: http://www.glam.ac.uk/home.html

|  | HND | Degree |
|---|---|---|
| No of courses | 4 | 21 |
| A-level score | 6 | 11 |
| GNVQ |  | M |
| SQA grades |  |  |
| BTEC |  | 5M |

UCAS code: G28
**University of Glasgow,** Glasgow G12 8QQ
tel: 0141 330 4575/4515; fax: 0141 330 4413
e-mail: admissions@mis.gla.ac.uk
www: http://www.gla.ac.uk/admissions

|  | HND | Degree |
|---|---|---|
| No of courses |  | 3 |
| A-level score |  | 18 |
| GNVQ |  | M |
| SQA grades |  | BBBB |
| BTEC |  | N |

UCAS code: G70
**University of Greenwich**
Avery Hill Campus, Mansion Site, Bexley Road
Eltham SE9 2PQ
tel: 0181 331 8044; fax: 0181 331 9856
e-mail: p.fisher@greenwich.ac.uk
www: http://www.gre.ac.uk/

|  | HND | Degree |
|---|---|---|
| No of courses | 1 | 3 |
| A-level score | 6 | 13 |
| GNVQ | P | M |
| SQA grades |  | BBB |
| BTEC | N | MO+ |

UCAS code: H06
**Halton College**
Kingsway, Widnes WA8 7QQ
tel: 0151 423 1391; fax: 0151 420 2408
e-mail: halton.college@cityscape.co.uk
www: http://www.cityscape.co.uk/users/aj75/index.ht

|  | HND | Degree |
|---|---|---|
| No of courses | 1 |  |
| A-level score | 2 |  |
| GNVQ |  |  |
| SQA grades |  |  |
| BTEC |  |  |

UCAS code: H36
**University of Hertfordshire**
Mercer Building, College Lane, Hatfield AL10 9AB
tel: 01707 284800; fax: 01707 284870
www: http://www.herts.ac.uk/

|  | HND | Degree |
|---|---|---|
| No of courses |  | 1 |
| A-level score |  | 14 |
| GNVQ |  |  |
| SQA grades |  |  |
| BTEC |  |  |

UCAS code: H60
**The University of Huddersfield**
Queensgate, Huddersfield HD1 3DH
tel: 01484 422288; fax: 01484 516151
e-mail: prospectus@hud.ac.uk
www: http://www.hud.ac.uk/

|  | HND | Degree |
|---|---|---|
| No of courses |  | 1 |
| A-level score |  | 12 |
| GNVQ |  | D |
| SQA grades |  | BBBC |
| BTEC |  | 6M |

UCAS code: H72
**The University of Hull**
Cottingham Road, Hull HU6 7RX
tel: 01482 466200; fax: 01482 442290
e-mail: admissions@admin.hull.ac.uk
www: http://www.hull.ac.uk/

|  | HND | Degree |
|---|---|---|
| No of courses |  | 4 |
| A-level score |  | 18 |
| GNVQ |  | M |
| SQA grades |  | BBBCC |
| BTEC |  | MO |

UCAS code: K48
**King Alfred's Winchester**
Winchester SO22 4NR
tel: 01962 841515; fax: 01962 827406
e-mail: admissions@wkac.ac.uk
www: http://www.wkac.ac.uk/

|  | HND | Degree |
|---|---|---|
| No of courses |  | 5 |
| A-level score |  | 14 |
| GNVQ |  | M |
| SQA grades |  | BCC |
| BTEC |  | 6M |

UCAS code: K84
**Kingston University,** River House, 53–57 High
Street, Kingston-upon-Thames KT1 1LQ
tel: 0181 547 2000; fax: 0181 547 7080
e-mail: d.milner-walker@kingston.ac.uk
www: http://www.kingston.ac.uk/

|  | HND | Degree |
|---|---|---|
| No of courses |  | 2 |
| A-level score |  | 18 |
| GNVQ |  |  |
| SQA grades |  |  |
| BTEC |  |  |

UCAS code: L23
**University of Leeds,** Leeds LS2 9JT
tel: 0113 233 2332; fax: 0113 233 2334
www: http://www.leeds.ac.uk/

|  | HND | Degree |
|---|---|---|
| No of courses |  | 2 |
| A-level score |  | 22 |
| GNVQ |  |  |
| SQA grades |  | ABBBB |
| BTEC |  |  |

UCAS code: L24
**Leeds, Trinity & All Saints University College**
Brownberrie Lane, Horsforth, Leeds LS18 5HD
tel: 0113 283 7123; fax: 0113 283 7200
www: http://www.tasc.ac.uk/

|  | HND | Degree |
|---|---|---|
| No of courses |  | 3 |
| A-level score |  | 20 |
| GNVQ |  |  |
| SQA grades |  | AABBB |
| BTEC |  | MO+ |

UCAS code: L27
**Leeds Metropolitan University**
Calverley Street, Leeds LS1 3HE
tel: 0113 283 3113; fax: 0113 283 3114
e-mail: course-enquiries@lmu.ac.uk
www: http://www.lmu.ac.uk/

|  | HND | Degree |
|---|---|---|
| No of courses | 1 | 4 |
| A-level score | 8 | 16 |
| GNVQ | M | D |
| SQA grades | BBC | BBBB |
| BTEC | 4M+2 | MO+ |

UCAS code: L39
**University of Lincolnshire & Humberside**
Milner Hall, Cottingham Road, Hull HU6 7RT
tel: 01482 440550; fax: 01482 463310
e-mail: marketing@ac.humber.uk
www: http://www.ulh.ac.uk/

|  | HND | Degree |
|---|---|---|
| No of courses |  | 1 |
| A-level score |  | 16 |
| GNVQ |  | D |
| SQA grades |  | BBCC |
| BTEC |  | 1M+3 |

UCAS code: L46
**Liverpool Hope University College**
PO Box 6, Stand Park Road, Liverpool L16 9JD
tel: 0151 291 3000; fax: 0151 291 3048
www: http://www.livhope.ac.uk/

|  | HND | Degree |
|---|---|---|
| No of courses |  | 14 |
| A-level score |  | 11 |
| GNVQ |  | P |
| SQA grades |  |  |
| BTEC |  | 8M |

UCAS code: L51
**Liverpool John Moores University**
Roscoe Court, 4 Rodney Street, Liverpool L1 2TZ
tel: 0151 231 5090/5091; fax: 0151 231 3194
e-mail: recruitment@livjm.ac.uk
www: http://www.livjm.ac.uk/

|  | HND | Degree |
|---|---|---|
| No of courses |  | 4 |
| A-level score |  | 16 |
| GNVQ |  |  |
| SQA grades |  | BBBB |
| BTEC |  | MO+ |

UCAS code: L53
**Llandrillo College (North Wales)**
Llandudno Road, Colwyn Bay LL28 4HZ
tel: 01492 546666; fax: 01492 543052
e-mail: admissions@llandrillo.ac.uk

|  | HND | Degree |
|---|---|---|
| No of courses | 1 |  |
| A-level score | 4 |  |
| GNVQ | P |  |
| SQA grades |  |  |
| BTEC | N |  |

UCAS code: L79
**Loughborough University**
Ashby Road, Loughborough LE11 3TU
tel: 01509 263171; fax: 01509 223905
e-mail: w.j.clarke@lboro.ac.uk
www: http://www.lboro.ac.uk/

|  | HND | Degree |
|---|---|---|
| No of courses |  | 8 |
| A-level score |  | 23 |
| GNVQ |  | D |
| SQA grades |  |  |
| BTEC |  |  |

UCAS code: L93
**University of Luton**
Park Square, Luton LU1 3JU
tel: 01582 489286; fax: 01582 489323
e-mail: pat.herber@luton.ac.uk.
www: http://www.luton.ac.uk/

|  | HND | Degree |
|---|---|---|
| No of courses | 2 | 6 |
| A-level score | 8 | 14 |
| GNVQ | M | D |
| SQA grades | BCCC | BBCC |
| BTEC | M | M+D |

UCAS code: M40
**The Manchester Metropolitan University**
All Saints, Manchester M15 6BH
tel: 0161 247 2966; fax: 0161 247 6311
e-mail: prospectus@mmu.ac.uk
www: http://www.mmu.ac.uk/

|  | HND | Degree |
|---|---|---|
| No of courses | 1 | 22 |
| A-level score | 4 | 14 |
| GNVQ | M | D |
| SQA grades | C | BBB |
| BTEC | 3M | 4M+1 |

UCAS code: M77
**Mid-Cheshire College**
Hartford Campus, Northwich CW8 1LJ
tel: 01606 74444; fax: 01606 75101
www: http://www.midchesh.u-net.com/

|  | HND | Degree |
|---|---|---|
| No of courses | 1 |  |
| A-level score | 2 |  |
| GNVQ |  |  |
| SQA grades |  |  |
| BTEC | 3M |  |

UCAS code: M80
**Middlesex University**
White Hart Lane, London N17 8HR
tel: 0181 362 5898; fax: 0181 362 5649
e-mail: admissions@mdx.ac.uk
www: http://www.mdx.ac.uk/

|  | HND | Degree |
|---|---|---|
| No of courses | 1 | 1 |
| A-level score | 8 | 12 |
| GNVQ | P | M |
| SQA grades |  |  |
| BTEC | N | 5M |

UCAS code: M90
**Moray House Institute of Education**
Holyrood Road, Edinburgh EH8 8AQ
tel: 0131 556 8455; fax: 0131 557 3458
www: http://www.mhie.ac.uk/

|  | HND | Degree |
|---|---|---|
| No of courses |  | 1 |
| A-level score |  | 14 |
| GNVQ |  |  |
| SQA grades |  | BBBC |
| BTEC |  |  |

UCAS code: N14
**Nene, University College Northampton**
Park Campus, Moulton Park, Northampton NN2 7AL
tel: 01604 735500; fax: 01604 720636
e-mail: admissions@nene.ac.uk
www: http://www.nene.ac.uk/

|  | HND | Degree |
|---|---|---|
| No of courses |  | 45 |
| A-level score |  | 11 |
| GNVQ |  | M |
| SQA grades |  | BBB |
| BTEC |  | 5M |

UCAS code: N23
**Newcastle College,** Ryehill Campus,
Scotswood Road, Newcastle upon Tyne NE4 7SA
tel: 0191 200 4110; fax: 0191 272 4297
e-mail: sdoughty@ncl-coll.ac.uk
www: http://www.ncl-coll.ac.uk/

|  | HND | Degree |
|---|---|---|
| No of courses | 1 |  |
| A-level score |  |  |
| GNVQ |  |  |
| SQA grades |  |  |
| BTEC |  |  |

UCAS code: N37
**University of Wales College Newport**
Caerleon Campus, PO Box 101, Newport NP6 1YH
tel: 01633 432432; fax: 01633 432850
e-mail: uic@newport.ac.uk
www: http://www.newport.ac.uk/

|  | HND | Degree |
|---|---|---|
| No of courses |  | 6 |
| A-level score |  | 10 |
| GNVQ |  | D |
| SQA grades |  |  |
| BTEC |  | M+D |

UCAS code: N49
**Nescot,** Reigate Road, Ewell, Epsom KT17 3DS
tel: 0181 394 1731; fax: 0181 394 3030
e-mail: lclewlow@nescot.ac.uk
www: http://www.nescot.ac.uk/

|  | HND | Degree |
|---|---|---|
| No of courses | 1 | 1 |
| A-level score | 4 | 8 |
| GNVQ | P | M |
| SQA grades |  |  |
| BTEC | 6M | N |

UCAS code: N56
**North East Wales Institute of Higher Education**
Plas Coch, Mold Road, Wrexham LL11 2AW
tel: 01978 290666; fax: 01978 290008
e-mail: k.mitchell@newi.ac.uk
www: http://www.newi.ac.uk/

|  | HND | Degree |
|---|---|---|
| No of courses |  | 35 |
| A-level score |  | 4 |
| GNVQ |  | M |
| SQA grades |  | BBB |
| BTEC |  | 3M |

UCAS code: N63
**University of North London**
166–220 Holloway Road, London N7 8DB
tel: 0171 753 5066; fax: 0171 753 5075
e-mail: admissions@unl.ac.uk
www: http://www.unl.ac.uk/

|  | HND | Degree |
|---|---|---|
| No of courses | 1 | 9 |
| A-level score | 8 | 12 |
| GNVQ |  | M |
| SQA grades | CCC |  |
| BTEC | 10M | 4M |

UCAS code: N77
**University of Northumbria at Newcastle**
Ellison Building, Ellison Place
Newcastle upon Tyne NE1 8ST
tel: 0191 227 4064; fax: 0191 227 3009
e-mail: rg.admissions@unn.ac.uk
www: http://www.unn.ac.uk/

|  | HND | Degree |
|---|---|---|
| No of courses |  | 3 |
| A-level score |  | 17 |
| GNVQ |  | D |
| SQA grades |  | BBBCC |
| BTEC |  | 1M+4 |

UCAS code: N91
**The Nottingham Trent University**
Burton Street, Nottingham NG1 4BU
tel: 0115 941 8418; fax: 0115 948 6063
www: http://www.ntu.ac.uk/

|  | HND | Degree |
|---|---|---|
| No of courses | 4 | 8 |
| A-level score | 8 | 16 |
| GNVQ |  |  |
| SQA grades | C | B |
| BTEC | MO |  |

UCAS code: O66
**Oxford Brookes University**
Gipsy Lane Campus, Headington, Oxford OX3 0BP
tel: 01865 483040; fax: 01865 483983
www: http://www.brookes.ac.uk/

|              | HND | Degree |
|--------------|-----|--------|
| No of courses |     | 64     |
| A-level score |     | 8      |
| GNVQ          |     | P      |
| SQA grades    |     |        |
| BTEC          |     |        |

UCAS code: P60
**University of Plymouth**
Drake Circus, Plymouth PL4 8AA
tel: 01752 232135; fax: 01752 232179
e-mail: c.todd@plymouth.ac.uk
www: http://www.plym.ac.uk/

|               | HND | Degree |
|---------------|-----|--------|
| No of courses | 2   | 1      |
| A-level score | 6   | 14     |
| GNVQ          | M   | M      |
| SQA grades    |     |        |
| BTEC          | MO  | MO     |

UCAS code: P80
**University of Portsmouth,** University House,
Winston Churchill Avenue, Portsmouth PO1 2UP
tel: 01705 876543; fax: 01705 843082
e-mail: admissions@reg.port.ac.uk
www: http://www.port.ac.uk/

|               | HND | Degree |
|---------------|-----|--------|
| No of courses |     | 5      |
| A-level score |     | 18     |
| GNVQ          |     | D      |
| SQA grades    |     | BBBB   |
| BTEC          |     | MO+    |

UCAS code: R24
**University College of Ripon & York St John**
Lord Mayor's Walk, York YO3 7EX
tel: 01904 616850; fax: 01904 616921
e-mail: l.waghorn@ucrysj.ac.uk
www: http://www.ucrysj.ac.uk/

|               | HND | Degree |
|---------------|-----|--------|
| No of courses |     | 7      |
| A-level score |     | 15     |
| GNVQ          |     | M      |
| SQA grades    |     | ABBB   |
| BTEC          |     | MO+    |

UCAS code: R48
**Roehampton Institute London**
Roehampton Lane, London SW15 5PU
tel: 0181 392 3000; fax: 0181 392 3220
e-mail: admissions@roehampton.ac.uk
www: http://www.roehampton.ac.uk/

|               | HND | Degree |
|---------------|-----|--------|
| No of courses |     | 30     |
| A-level score |     | 12     |
| GNVQ          |     | M      |
| SQA grades    |     | BBC    |
| BTEC          |     | 3D     |

UCAS code: S03
**The University of Salford**
Salford M5 4WT
tel: 0161 295 5461/5509; fax: 0161 745 3126
e-mail: a.l.farrell@university-management.salford.ac.uk
www: http://www.salford.ac.uk/homepage.html

|               | HND | Degree |
|---------------|-----|--------|
| No of courses |     | 2      |
| A-level score |     | 15     |
| GNVQ          |     |        |
| SQA grades    |     |        |
| BTEC          |     |        |

UCAS code: S10
**University College Scarborough**
Filey Road, Scarborough YO11 3AZ
tel: 01723 362392; fax: 01723 370815
e-mail: registry@ucscarb.ac.uk
www: http://www.ucscarb.ac.uk/

|               | HND | Degree |
|---------------|-----|--------|
| No of courses |     | 1      |
| A-level score |     |        |
| GNVQ          |     | P      |
| SQA grades    |     |        |
| BTEC          |     |        |

UCAS code: S21
**Sheffield Hallam University**
Surrey Building, Sheffield S1 1WB
tel: 0114 253 3490; fax: 0114 253 4023
e-mail: c.arnold@shu.ac.uk
www: http://www.shu.ac.uk/

|               | HND | Degree |
|---------------|-----|--------|
| No of courses | 1   | 5      |
| A-level score |     | 16     |
| GNVQ          |     | D      |
| SQA grades    |     |        |
| BTEC          |     | 6M+4   |

UCAS code: S22
**Sheffield College**
PO Box 345, Sheffield S2 2YY
tel: 0114 260 3007; fax: 0114 260 2301

|               | HND   | Degree |
|---------------|-------|--------|
| No of courses | 1     |        |
| A-level score |       |        |
| GNVQ          |       |        |
| SQA grades    |       |        |
| BTEC          | 3M+2  |        |

UCAS code: S23
**Shrewsbury College of Arts & Technology**
London Road, Shrewsbury SY2 7PR
tel: 01743 342342; fax: 01743 241684
e-mail: mail@s-cat.ac.uk

|               | HND | Degree |
|---------------|-----|--------|
| No of courses | 1   |        |
| A-level score |     |        |
| GNVQ          | P   |        |
| SQA grades    |     |        |
| BTEC          |     |        |

UCAS code: S24
**University College of St Martin, Lancaster & Cumbria,** Bowerham Road, Lancaster LA1 3JD
tel: 01524 384444; fax: 01524 384567
e-mail: admissions@ucsm.ac.uk
www: http://www.ucsm.ac.uk/

|  | HND | Degree |
|---|---|---|
| No of courses |  | 23 |
| A-level score |  | 11 |
| GNVQ |  | P |
| SQA grades |  | BBBB |
| BTEC |  | 3M+3 |

UCAS code: S26
**Solihull College**
Blossomfield Road, Solihull B91 1SB
tel: 0121 678 7001/2; fax: 0121 678 7200
e-mail: enquiries@staff.solihull.ac.uk
www: http://www.solihull.ac.uk/

|  | HND | Degree |
|---|---|---|
| No of courses | 1 | 1 |
| A-level score | 2 | 8 |
| GNVQ | P | M |
| SQA grades |  |  |
| BTEC | N | M+2 |

UCAS code: S27
**University of Southampton**
Southampton SO17 1BJ
tel: 01703 595000; fax: 01703 593037
e-mail: prospenq@soton.ac.uk
www: http://www.soton.ac.uk

|  | HND | Degree |
|---|---|---|
| No of courses |  | 11 |
| A-level score |  | 12 |
| GNVQ |  |  |
| SQA grades |  |  |
| BTEC |  |  |

UCAS code: S28
**Somerset College of Arts & Technology**
Wellington Road, Taunton TA1 5AX
tel: 01823 366366; fax: 01823 355418
www: http://www.zynet.co.uk/scat1/

|  | HND | Degree |
|---|---|---|
| No of courses | 1 |  |
| A-level score |  |  |
| GNVQ |  |  |
| SQA grades |  |  |
| BTEC |  |  |

UCAS code: S30
**Southampton Institute**
East Park Terrace, Southampton SO14 0YN
tel: 01703 319039; fax: 01703 334161
e-mail: MS@Solent.ac.uk
www: http://www.solent.ac.uk/

|  | HND | Degree |
|---|---|---|
| No of courses | 1 | 2 |
| A-level score | 6 | 9 |
| GNVQ | M | M |
| SQA grades | CCCC | CCCC |
| BTEC | MO | MO |

UCAS code: S33
**South Bank University**
103 Borough Road, London SE1 0AA
tel: 0171 815 8158; fax: 0171 815 8273
e-mail: enrol@sbu.ac.uk
www: http://www.sbu.ac.uk/

|  | HND | Degree |
|---|---|---|
| No of courses |  | 20 |
| A-level score |  | 12 |
| GNVQ |  | M |
| SQA grades |  |  |
| BTEC |  | N |

UCAS code: S38
**Southwark College,** Surrey Docks Centre, Drummond Road, London SE16 4EE
tel: 0171 815 1600; fax: 0171 815 1525
e-mail: ucas@southwark.ac.uk
www: www.southwark.ac.uk

|  | HND | Degree |
|---|---|---|
| No of courses | 2 |  |
| A-level score | 2 |  |
| GNVQ |  |  |
| SQA grades |  |  |
| BTEC |  |  |

UCAS code: S51
**St Helens College**
Brook Street, St Helens, Merseyside WA10 1PZ
tel: 01744 623338; fax: 01744 623421
www: http://www.sthelens.mernet.org.uk/

|  | HND | Degree |
|---|---|---|
| No of courses | 2 |  |
| A-level score | 2 |  |
| GNVQ | P |  |
| SQA grades |  |  |
| BTEC | N |  |

UCAS code: S59
**The University College of St Mark & St John**
Derriford Road, Plymouth PL19 9AL
tel: 01752 636827; fax: 01752 636849
www: http://194.80.168.100/

|  | HND | Degree |
|---|---|---|
| No of courses |  | 12 |
| A-level score |  | 10 |
| GNVQ |  | M |
| SQA grades |  | CCCC |
| BTEC |  | MO |

UCAS code: S64
**St Mary's University College,** Waldegrave Road, Strawberry Hill, Twickenham TW1 4SW
tel: 0181 240 4000; fax: 0181 240 4255
www: http://www.smuc.ac.uk/

|  | HND | Degree |
|---|---|---|
| No of courses |  | 15 |
| A-level score |  | 9 |
| GNVQ |  |  |
| SQA grades |  | BBBB |
| BTEC |  |  |

UCAS code: S72
**Staffordshire University**
College Road, Stoke-on-Trent ST4 2DE
tel: 01782 292752; fax: 01782 745422
e-mail: admissions@staffs.ac.uk
www: http://www.staffs.ac.uk/

|  | HND | Degree |
|---|---|---|
| No of courses | 11 |  |
| A-level score | 15 |  |
| GNVQ | D |  |
| SQA grades | BBCC |  |
| BTEC | 2M+4 |  |

UCAS code: S75
**The University of Stirling,** Stirling FK9 4LA
tel: 01786 467044; fax: 01786 466800
e-mail: admnl@stir.ac.uk
www: http://www.stir.ac.uk/

|  | HND | Degree |
|---|---|---|
| No of courses |  | 7 |
| A-level score |  | 21 |
| GNVQ |  | M |
| SQA grades |  | BBBB |
| BTEC |  | MO+ |

UCAS code: S76
**Stockport College of Further & Higher Education**
Wellington Road South, Stockport SK1 3UQ
tel: 0161 958 3416; fax: 0161 958 3305
www: http://www.stockport.ac.uk/

|  | HND | Degree |
|---|---|---|
| No of courses | 1 |  |
| A-level score | 2 |  |
| GNVQ | P |  |
| SQA grades |  |  |
| BTEC |  |  |

UCAS code: S78
**The University of Strathclyde,** McCance Building,
16 Richmond Street, Glasgow G1 1XQ
tel: 0141 548 2814; fax: 0141 552 7362
e-mail: j.foulds@mis.strath.ac.uk
www: http://www.strath.ac.uk/Campus/ prospect/info/i

|  | HND | Degree |
|---|---|---|
| No of courses |  | 2 |
| A-level score |  | 14 |
| GNVQ |  |  |
| SQA grades |  | AAB |
| BTEC |  |  |

UCAS code: S84
**University of Sunderland,** St Mary's Building,
Chester Road, Sunderland SR1 3SD
tel: 0191 515 3000; fax: 0191 515 3805
e-mail: student-helpline@sunderland.ac.uk
www: http://www.sunderland.ac.uk/

|  | HND | Degree |
|---|---|---|
| No of courses |  | 4 |
| A-level score |  | 18 |
| GNVQ |  | M |
| SQA grades |  | BBCC |
| BTEC |  | 3M+2 |

UCAS code: S93
**University of Wales Swansea**
Singleton Park, Swansea SA2 8PP
tel: 01792 295111; fax: 01792 295110
e-mail: admissions@swan.ac.uk
www: http://www.swan.ac.uk/

|  | HND | Degree |
|---|---|---|
| No of courses | 1 | 1 |
| A-level score |  | 20 |
| GNVQ |  |  |
| SQA grades |  | ABBBB |
| BTEC |  | 1M+5 |

UCAS code: S96
**Swansea Institute of Higher Education**
Mount Pleasant, Swansea SA1 6ED
tel: 01792 481000; fax: 01792 481263
e-mail: enquiry@sihe.ac.uk
www: http://www.sihe.ac.uk/home.html

|  | HND | Degree |
|---|---|---|
| No of courses |  | 1 |
| A-level score |  | 4 |
| GNVQ |  | P |
| SQA grades |  | CCCC |
| BTEC |  | N |

UCAS code: T20
**University of Teesside**
Borough Road, Middlesbrough TS1 3BA
tel: 01642 218121; fax: 01642 384201
e-mail: H.Cummins@tees.ac.uk
www: http://www@tees.ac.uk/

|  | HND | Degree |
|---|---|---|
| No of courses |  | 24 |
| A-level score |  | 14 |
| GNVQ |  | M |
| SQA grades |  | BBCC |
| BTEC |  |  |

UCAS code: T40
**Thames Valley University**
St Mary's Road, Ealing, London W5 5RF
tel: 0181 579 5000; fax: 0181 231 2900
e-mail: christine.marchant@tvu.ac.uk
www: http://www.tvu.ac.uk/

|  | HND | Degree |
|---|---|---|
| No of courses |  | 1 |
| A-level score |  | 8 |
| GNVQ |  | M |
| SQA grades |  | CCC |
| BTEC |  | MO |

UCAS code: T80
**Trinity College Carmarthen**
College Road, Carmarthen SA31 3EP
tel: 01267 676767; fax: 01267 676766

|  | HND | Degree |
|---|---|---|
| No of courses |  | 12 |
| A-level score |  | 4 |
| GNVQ |  |  |
| SQA grades |  |  |
| BTEC |  |  |

UCAS code: U20
**University of Ulster,** University House,
Cromore Road, Coleraine BT52 1SA
tel: 01265 44141; fax: 01265 324908
e-mail: ja.elliott@ulst.ac.uk
www: http://www.ulst.ac.uk/

|  | HND | Degree |
| --- | --- | --- |
| No of courses |  | 1 |
| A-level score |  | 22 |
| GNVQ |  | D |
| SQA grades |  | ABBB |
| BTEC |  | MO+ |

UCAS code: W17
**University College Warrington,** Padgate Campus,
Fearnhead, Warrington WA2 0DB
tel: 01925 494494; fax: 01925 494289
e-mail: registry.he@warr.ac.uk
www: http://www.warr.ac.uk/unicoll.html

|  | HND | Degree |
| --- | --- | --- |
| No of courses |  | 2 |
| A-level score |  | 11 |
| GNVQ |  |  |
| SQA grades |  |  |
| BTEC |  |  |

UCAS code: W40
**West Herts College, Watford**
Hempstead Road, Watford WD1 3EZ
tel: 01923 812565; fax: 01923 812540

|  | HND | Degree |
| --- | --- | --- |
| No of courses | 1 |  |
| A-level score |  |  |
| GNVQ |  |  |
| SQA grades |  |  |
| BTEC |  |  |

UCAS code: W43
**Westhill College of Higher Education**
Weoley Park Road, Selly Oak, Birmingham B29 6LL
tel: 0121 415 2206; fax: 0121 415 5399
e-mail: c.evans@westhill.ac.uk
www: http://www.westhill.ac.uk/

|  | HND | Degree |
| --- | --- | --- |
| No of courses |  | 1 |
| A-level score |  | 12 |
| GNVQ |  | M |
| SQA grades |  |  |
| BTEC |  | 4M+2 |

UCAS code: W50
**University of Westminster,** Metford House, 15–18
Clipstone Street, London W1M 8JS
tel: 0171 911 5000; fax: 0171 911 5858
www: http://www.wmin.ac.uk/

|  | HND | Degree |
| --- | --- | --- |
| No of courses |  | 1 |
| A-level score |  |  |
| GNVQ |  |  |
| SQA grades |  |  |
| BTEC |  |  |

UCAS code: W67
**Wigan & Leigh College**
PO Box 53, Parson's Walk, Wigan WN1 1RR
tel: 01942 501528; fax: 01942 501533

|  | HND | Degree |
| --- | --- | --- |
| No of courses | 1 |  |
| A-level score | 2 |  |
| GNVQ |  |  |
| SQA grades |  |  |
| BTEC | N |  |

UCAS code: W75
**University of Wolverhampton**
Compton Park Campus
Wolverhampton WV3 9DX
tel: 01902 321000; fax: 01902 323744
e-mail: a.fitzpatrick@wlv.ac.uk
www: http://www.wlv.ac.uk/

|  | HND | Degree |
| --- | --- | --- |
| No of courses |  | 2 |
| A-level score |  | 14 |
| GNVQ |  | M |
| SQA grades |  | BBBB |
| BTEC |  | 4M |

UCAS code: W80
**University College Worcester**
Henwick Grove, Worcester WR2 6AJ
tel: 01905 855111; fax: 01905 855132
www: http://www.worc.ac.uk/worcs.html

|  | HND | Degree |
| --- | --- | --- |
| No of courses | 1 | 11 |
| A-level score | 4 | 12 |
| GNVQ | M | M |
| SQA grades |  |  |
| BTEC |  |  |

UCAS code: Y80
**Yorkshire Coast College of Further & Higher Education**
Lady Edith's Drive, Scalby Road
Scarborough YO12 5RN
tel: 01723 372105; fax: 01723 501918
e-mail: admissions@ycoastco.ac.uk
www: http://www.cbconnect.co.uk/ycc.html

|  | HND | Degree |
| --- | --- | --- |
| No of courses | 1 |  |
| A-level score | 2 |  |
| GNVQ | P |  |
| SQA grades |  |  |
| BTEC | N |  |

# USEFUL ADDRESSES

**British Council of Physical Education**
PO Box 6, Woolton Road
Liverpool L16 8ND
0151 737 3461

**City & Guilds**
1 Giltspur Street
London EC1A 9DD
0171 294 2468

**Institute of Groundsmanship**
19–23 Church Street
Wolverton, Milton Keynes
Bucks MK12 5LG
01908 312511

**Institute of Leisure and Amenity Management**
ILAM House, Lower Basildon
Reading, Berks RG8 9NE
01491 874800

**Institute of Sport and Recreational Management**
Giffard House, 36–38 Sherrard Street
Melton Mowbray, Leics LE13 1XJ
01664 565531

**National Council for the Training of Journalists**
Latton Bush Centre, Southern Way
Harlow, Essex CM18 7BL
01279 430009

**Skill: National Bureau for Students with Disabilities**
336 Brixton Road
London SW9 7AA
0171 274 0565

**Sports and Recreation Industry Training Organisation**
24 Stevenson Way
London NW1 2HD
0171 388 7755

**The Sports Council of England**
16 Woburn Place
London WC1H 0QP
0171 273 1500

**The Sports Council of Northern Ireland**
House of Sport
Upper Malone Road
Belfast BT9 5LA
01232 381222

**The Sports Council of Scotland**
Caledonia House
South Gyle
Edinburgh EH12 9DQ
0131 317 7200

**The Sports Council of Wales**
Sophia Gardens
Cardiff CF1 9SW
01222 300500

**Universities and Colleges Admissions Service (UCAS)**
Fulton House
Jessop Avenue
Cheltenham
Glos GL50 3SH
Applicant enquiries: 01242 227788
General enquiries: 01242 222444
e-mail: enq@ucas.ac.uk
website: http://www.ucas.ac.uk